D0404909

An Introduction to the Metaphysics of St. Thomas Aquinas

AN
INTRODUCTION
TO THE
METAPHYSICS
OF ST. THOMAS
AQUINAS

Texts Selected, Translated, and with a Preface by
JAMES F. ANDERSON
University of Notre Dame
with a new Introduction by W. Norris Clarke, S.J.

Gateway Editions
REGNERY PUBLISHING, INC.
WASHINGTON, D.C.

Copyright © 1953 Regnery Publishing, Inc.
Introduction Copyright © 1997 Regnery Publishing, Inc.

All rights reserved. No part of this publication may be reproduced or trans-
mitted in any form or by any means electronic or mechanical, including pho-
tocopy, recording, or any information storage and retrieval system now known
or to be invented, without permission in writing from the publisher, except by
a reviewer who wishes to quote brief passages in connection with a review
written for inclusion in a magazine, newspaper, or broadcast.

Library of Congress Cataloging-in-Publication Data

Thomas, Aquinas, Saint, 1225?–1274.
    [Selections. English. 1997]
    An introduction to the metaphysics of St. Thomas Aquinas / texts
selected and translated by James F. Anderson ; with a new introduction
by W. Norris Clarke.
        p.   cm.
    Includes bibliographical references.
    Originally published: c1953
    ISBN 0-89526-420-X
    1. Metaphysics—Early works to 1800. I. Anderson, James Francis,
1910– . II. Title.
B765.T52E5 1997
110–dc21   97–8643
                                                  CIP

Published in the United States by
Regnery Publishing, Inc.
An Eagle Publishing Company
422 First Street, SE
Washington, DC 20003

Distributed to the trade by
National Book Network
4720-A Boston Way
Lanham, MD 20706

Printed on acid-free paper.
Manufactured in the United States of America

10 9 8 7 6 5 4 3 2

Books are available in quantity for promotional or premium use. Write to
Director of Special Sales, Regnery Publishing, Inc., 422 First Street, SE, Suite
300, Washington, DC 20003, for information on discounts and terms or call
(202) 546-5005.

To Lois

CONTENTS

INTRODUCTION

S INCE THIS COLLECTION of texts from St. Thomas was first published in 1953, it has proved of great service to teachers of
philosophy giving introductory courses on St. Thomas at all
levels. It is now out of print, and the original editor, James
Anderson, has passed away; so it has been judged appropriate to issue a new edition, with the texts themselves unchanged but with a
new Preface. It was also judged advisable to include a considerably
more ample explanation of what metaphysics and the study of being mean, and their significance for the study of philosophy and the
intellectual life in general. When Prof. Anderson first published this
collection, it was still the heyday of Thomistic philosophy as the lin-
gua franca of the community of American Catholic higher educa-
tion institutions and seminaries, and he did not feel the need to jus-
tify the study of metaphysics or even explain at great length what it
meant.

The situation is quite different today, forty-four years later, when
Thomism (outside of seminaries) can no longer be taken as the
common framework of thought in most American Catholic col-
leges and universities—and even less in the wider academic world,
where the predominant schools of philosophical thought are either
indifferent to metaphysical thinking (in the classical systematic sense
in which St. Thomas and Aristotle take it) or, more often, positively
sceptical or hostile toward it. Thus, "metaphysics" today, in the
contemporary academic world (outside the Aristotelian,
Thomistic-Scholastic, and Whiteheadian traditions), as is evident

from the textbooks and anthologies bearing that name, now means not the systematic study of being and the properties and laws applying to all beings as being, but rather a grab bag of diverse problems whose only common bond is that they cannot be solved by science, phenomenology, or other specialized philosophical techniques, e.g., freedom of the will, realism-idealism, the mind-body problem, the existence of God, and the like.

METAPHYSICS FOR ST. THOMAS

Metaphysics for St. Thomas—as for Aristotle, the medieval, and the classical modern tradition in general (whether they practiced it or opposed it)—was the foundational philosophical discipline, the foundational "science" in the broad Aristotelian meaning of "science" as "certain knowledge through causes" in whatever domain. Upon this science depended—at least implicitly—all other sciences for their ultimate presuppositions and basic guiding principles. Thus, just as the other particular philosophical disciplines seek to understand their particular subject matter, e.g., philosophy of man, philosophy of nature, etc., through the ultimate causes within their particular domain, so there must be one foundational science which seeks to understand all reality, all beings, in terms of the universal properties, laws, and ultimate causes of *being* as such.

Such a science was originally called "metaphysics" shortly after Aristotle's own time (who was the first one formally to identify and define the science) because, as the architectonic" (or "wisdom") science ordering all others, it was appropriate that it should be studied after (meta) "physics," or "philosophy of nature" (from *physis,* meaning "nature" in Greek), which included the whole natural world of change available to human experience. (The actual name, however, of *Metaphysics* ("That Which Comes after Physics") was first given simply to indicate the place of these books in the official collection and publication in Rome of the works of Aristotle by Andronicus of Rhodes some 150 years after Aristotle's death in 324 B.C.)

Metaphysics is the foundational science for all others, first, because all other particular sciences presuppose their particular subject matter as *already existing,* as *given* with its particular nature, and then go on to study this nature with its characteristic properties, laws of operation, etc. Secondly, not one of these particular sciences can, by its own principles, study what is common to it and to all other sciences. Above all, no particular science can even raise the question of why there actually is a real universe at all to be studied. Hence, under pain of frustrating the built-in natural desire of the mind to know reality in its fullness, there must be one foundational, architectonic philosophical discipline or science whose proper object is the study of *being as being,* that is, all beings precisely insofar as they are beings, as they possess being, together with the characteristic properties and laws that belong to them as beings, and especially the ultimate cause(s) which explain why they *are,* and are *what* they are. It is this systematic study that St. Thomas calls "metaphysics."

If St. Thomas were to come back among us and confront those contemporary philosophers who either ignore metaphysics or deny its possibility, I think he would courteously but firmly point out to them that no matter what philosophical positions they hold or what method they use, they must all presuppose or take for granted the actual existence of themselves as philosophers posing the questions and dialoguing with each other, as well as of the world they are trying to describe or explain. Hence they are all at least implicitly presupposing some kind of metaphysical view on what it means to be and what is necessarily implied by that. And it is much wiser to subject this most fundamental level of knowledge to explicit critical reflection than merely take it for granted without conscious awareness or critical control. He would also point out, to which the whole history of modern philosophy bears eloquent witness, that every attempt to deny the possibility of metaphysics rests on some prior arbitrarily restrictive epistemology or theory of knowledge. This claim, which I believe can be cogently enough demonstrated from the history of philosophy, is illuminating for understanding one of the key differences between ancient-medieval and modern Western philosophy; but we cannot pursue this exploration here.

THE STRUCTURE OF THOMISTIC METAPHYSICS

The *subject matter* of metaphysics is *being* insofar as it is given to us in our common human experience as that which is to be understood and explained, rendered as fully intelligible as is possible to us human philosophers, using our natural reason alone. Hence, it is the whole world of finite, changing, at least partly material, beings open to our experience and intellectual investigation, considered precisely insofar as they are *beings*. We can then extend the conclusions discovered here to the entire realm of real being as such, insofar as they can be shown to be necessary properties or implications of the very intelligibility of being as such.

There are two main *divisions* of this inquiry. The *first* is the inquiry into the meaning of being; into the transcendental attributes proper to all beings as such, such as unity, activity, truth, goodness, beauty; into the divisions running through the whole spectrum of finite, changing being, such as act and potency; and finally into the central problem of the domain of real being as irreducibly one and many: that is, how every being is both similar to every other in that it participates in being because it *is,* and yet there are many distinct beings in that this one is *not* that one. The *second division* is the inquiry into the ultimate cause(s) or Source of all being, in that the entire realm of finite and changing beings is discovered to be not self-sufficient, self-explanatory, that is, not adequate to render intelligible its own actual existence, and hence requires an ultimate self-sufficient First Cause, which for St. Thomas is God, together with the attributes which must necessarily belong to this being if it is to fulfill its necessary role in the intelligibility of being.

This second division of metaphysics, the search for the First Cause or Ultimate Source of all being, which for St. Thomas was the necessary crown and completion of metaphysics itself, was later divided, because of its length and importance, into a distinct philosophical discipline called "natural theology," or "philosophy of God," distinct from the first division, now called "general metaphysics." The present collection of texts does not cover this part of Thomistic metaphysics, the philosophical treatise on God, the reason being that St. Thomas himself has given us his own explicit and fully developed exposition of this in the first part of his two great *Summae,* the *Summa Theologiae* and the *Summa contra Gentes,* especially the former, Part I, Questions 1-26, 44-49, 103-119, in easily available English translations. Our collection covers only the *first division* of Thomistic metaphysics, as outlined above, covering the meaning of being, the necessary properties belonging to all beings as such, and the intrinsic constitutive principles of all finite beings. The reason for focusing on this first part of metaphysics is that St. Thomas himself has left us no systematic, properly philosophical treatise of his own, laying out his own personal thought as to the content and properly philosophical ordering of this material. One must reconstruct it from two sources: from his Commentaries on Aristotle, on Boethius, and on the Pseudo-Dionysius, with whom he generally agrees, but whose texts he unobtrusively interprets wherever necessary to fit his own thought; and from his own independent philosophical and theological works, in which his own mature philosophical-theological synthesis shines forth most clearly and fully.

St. Thomas distinguishes clearly enough his philosophical from his theological argumentation, so that it is quite possible to extract his basic philosophical positions from within his larger theological treatises, as Thomists have traditionally done down the ages. But it requires delicate, careful work, leaving considerable room for disagreements on certain particular points, especially as regards the order of development which best reflects the "authentic mind" of Aquinas himself, and how the Aristotelian dimension of his thought fits in coherently with his adaptation of it to Christian thought and also to his significant borrowings from the Neoplatonic metaphysical tradition available to him through St. Augustine, Pseudo-Dionysius, and others.

The only strictly philosophical treatises of his own that he has left us are *On the Principles of Nature,* a brief exposition of a strictly Aristotelian philosophy of nature, in terms of the first principles of change—act and potency, form and matter, and the four causes—without entering into a discussion of the wider dimension of being as such and its more universal properties and principles, let alone its ultimate causes. The second treatise, *On Being and Essence,* is indeed a properly metaphysical one—and a very valuable one indeed—but it limits itself to a discussion of the relations between the real and the logical order and the concepts proper to each, and then to the basic metaphysical structure proper to each of the three great levels of being in the universe: divine being, angelic being, (purely spiritual beings with no matter of any kind), and beings composed of form and matter (the world of our direct human experience). The central distinction between essence and the act of existence is introduced to explain the diversity within unity of the whole order of being, but there is no discussion of the transcendental properties of all beings, nor of the attributes of God, nor of other important points necessary to an adequate exposition of Thomistic metaphysics as a whole, such as the doctrine of efficient and final causality. It should be noted that neither does the present collection include treatment of these extrinsic causes of being, the efficient and final causes, for the reason that they provide the necessary introduction to the search for the ultimate Source of all being in the second division of metaphysics, which is not treated here.

The Meaning of *"Being"* for St. Thomas

The subject of metaphysics for St. Thomas, following Aristotle, is *being qua being,* that is, all beings, precisely insofar as they are beings, possess *being.* Since St. Thomas's understanding of being goes far beyond that of Aristotle, some elaboration is called for here. "A being," (used without qualification) means for him *that which is,* in the real order. The *that which* signifies what a thing is, its essence or nature, responding to the question, *"What* is it?" The *is* signifies the act of existing, or active presence, which posits the *what* in the real order, outside of nothingness, responding to the question, *"Is* it?", or "Does it *exist?"* It is in the interpretation of the *is* that St. Thomas goes well beyond his master. Aristotle and other philosophers, both before and after Aquinas, certainly recognized the significance of the *is* as signifying the *fact* of existence, as does ordinary language, and worked out explanations of how things came into being and passed out of it. But it had no further role to play in the inner metaphysical structure of beings themselves. St. Thomas penetrates further, beyond this mere *fact* of existence as affirmed by a knower, to the inner *act* of existence *within* the being itself, which is the ultimate *ground* for this affirmation of fact. This inner act of existence—which St. Thomas calls the *esse* or "to-be" of a being, that which makes a being precisely to be a *be*-ing—is not a *what,* an essence or nature, making a being to be *this kind* of being. It is, rather, an *active presence* which posits the entire essence, with all its properties, in the real order of actual existence, making it actually to be what it is.

In this way of looking at beings, the whole center of gravity of metaphysical explanation shifts from essence, *what* a being is, to the deeper level of the *act of existence* which alone gives actuality and value to everything within the being, both to its essence and all its attributes. Existence itself now turns out to be the central core and reservoir of all positivity and perfection of any kind within the order of real being. All the vast multiplicity and diversity of beings in the universe are now revealed as so many diverse modes of participation, through limiting essence, in the one great central source of all actuality and perfection, existence itself, which exists in its pure unparticipated, unlimited state in God alone, as the unique infinite Source of all being, not constricted within the bounds of any limiting essence, but pure subsistent *Esse* or Act of Existence, in all its inexhaustible richness and fullness.

These are the full implications of the famous Thomistic metaphysical doctrine of the "real distinction between essence and existence" in all beings save One, a distinction whose basic elements are set forth in terse and condensed form in the texts found here under Chapter III, Section 3. This powerfully integrated metaphysical vision of all reality as both One and Many is without a doubt St. Thomas's most original and significant contribution to the history of Western philosophy, one without close parallel in any philosophical thinker either before or after him. That is why this unique metaphysical vision centered around participation in the act of existence has been aptly called "existential Thomism" or "Thomistic existentialism," and why it is quite inaccurate and misleading to identify St. Thomas as simply a disciple of Aristotle, as some tend to do.

BEING AS ACTIVE AND SELF-COMMUNICATIVE

There is one aspect of being as understood by St. Thomas that is not included in the original selection of texts by Prof. Anderson, which are here reproduced unchanged. That is the dynamic character of every real being as tending naturally to pour over into *self-communicating action.* The full meaning of "being" now becomes not just that which is *actually present,* as standing out from nothingness, but *actively present* to other beings, opening out to them to form a network of interacting beings, bound to each other by relations of giving and receiving, acting and being acted upon, which we call the *universe,* that is, the unified system of all real beings (the term "universe" comes from the Latin *universum,* which means "turned toward unity").

St. Thomas comes to this conclusion, as he develops it throughout his works, by a kind of induction, showing how it is in fact manifested on all the different levels of being, including the divine (known not just by reason from creation, but also by Christian revelation of the nature of God as tri-personal self-communicating love, proceeding from Father, to Son, to Holy Spirit). But one can also show, by a simple metaphysical reflection or thought experiment, that this is not just a beautiful and rich way of looking at being, but a necessary one, if there is to be a universe at all. Let us suppose that there were some real being, actually present, but with no action whatsoever. What follows? First, it could not be *known* by any other being (except its Creator), since it would not manifest itself in any way, even by reacting, which is a form of action. Secondly, it would make no real *difference* at all in the world, to anything, but would be locked away in total self-isolation. In a word, it would be *indistinguishable from nothingness* by the rest of the universe, hence, might just as well not be at all. Any such being could not be a part of our universe, or any universe; and if all beings were such there simply would not be a universe at all. This is certainly not the universe that we know and live in, which is one where beings make a *difference* to each other, and are therefore self-manifesting through action; and it is not clear that a universe of non-acting beings could really be intelligible at all.

The implications of this understanding of being are very rich for understanding *personal being,* which for St. Thomas is the highest expression of being, "that which is most perfect in all of nature." It follows that the fullness of being can in the last analysis be found only in *persons in communion.* (I have developed this point more fully, with the supporting texts, in my little book, *Person and Being,* Milwaukee: Marquette University Press, 1993.) The sources of St. Thomas's doctrine derive from his own synthesis, inspired partly by Aristotle, partly by the ancient Neoplatonic doctrine of the "self-diffusiveness of the Good," as handed down to St. Thomas principally by the Pseudo-Dionysius (probably a Syrian-Christian monk of around the sixth century, who was believed to be Dionysius, the original disciple of St. Paul from Athens, up to the middle of the nineteenth century).

St. Thomas transposed the Dionysian doctrine into the "self-diffusiveness of being," since the good itself was rooted, for him, in the act of existence, the ultimate ground of all value and perfection. Since this important aspect of St. Thomas's understanding of being had not yet been given much stress by American Thomists at the time Prof. Anderson published his collection (1953), I have added on the following texts, which would fit in nicely right after Chapter II, Section 2, on "The Meaning of Being":

1. From the very fact that something exists in act, it is active. *Summa contra Gentes,* I, ch. 43.

2. Active power follows upon being in act, for anything acts in consequence of being in act. *Summa c. Gent.,* II, ch. 7.

3. Each and every thing abounds in the power of acting *(abundat in virtute agendi)* just insofar as it exists in act. *De Potentia,* q. 2, art. 2.

4. It is the nature of every actuality to communicate itself insofar as it is possible. Hence every agent acts according as it exists in actuality. *De Potentia,* q. 2, art. 1.

5. It follows upon the superabundance proper to perfection as such that the perfection which something has it can communicate

to another. Communication follows upon the very intelligibility (or meaning, *ratio*) of actuality. Hence every form is of itself communicable. *Summa c. Gent.,* III, ch. 64.

6. Natural things have a natural inclination not only toward their own proper good, to acquire it, if not possessed, and if possessed, to rest therein; but also to diffuse their own goodness among others as far as is possible. Hence, we see that every agent, insofar as it exists in act and possesses some perfection, produces something similar to itself. It pertains, therefore, to the nature of the will to communicate to others as far as possible the good possessed; and especially does this pertain to the divine will, from which all perfection is derived in some kind of likeness. Hence, if natural things, insofar as they are perfect, communicate their goodness to others, much more does it pertain to the divine will to communicate by likeness its own goodness to others as far as possible. *Summa Theologiae,* I, q. 19, art. 2.

7. Every substance exists for the sake of its operation. *Summa Theol.,* I, q. 105, art. 5.

8. Each and every thing shows forth that it exists for the sake of its operation; indeed, operation is the ultimate perfection of each thing. *Summa c. Gent.,* III, ch. 113.

9. The operation of a thing manifests both its substance [essence] and its existence. *Summa c. Gent.,* II, ch. 79.

10. The operation of a thing shows forth is power, which in turn points to [or points out: *indicat*] its essence. *Summa c. Gent.,* II, ch. 94.

11. The substantial forms of things, which, according as they are in themselves, are unknown to us, become known through their accidental properties. *Summa Theol.,* I, q. 77, art. 1, ad 7um.

The Transcendental Properties of All Beings

Prof. Anderson devotes almost half of his book to what he calls simply "The Transcendentals," without further explanation. Some further explication of this technical term is needed for those who are not Thomistic scholars. The term refers to that small number of attributes, or properties, that belong to *all beings* without exception, including God, and are identical with being itself, under some aspect. They are called "transcendental" because they transcend (from the Latin *transcendere*: to climb over) or leap over all boundaries and divisions between different kinds of being; they are not limited to any one being or kind of being but apply—analogously, of course—to all beings. According to a long tradition, the number is three: every being is *one, true* (intelligible), and *good*. Later medieval authors, including St. Thomas, and following Pseudo-Dionysius, add on *beautiful.* In practice he also includes *active,* as we have seen above, but he never includes this as part of his official list, since it was not in fact traditional. It should be noted that the term "transcendental" does not have the same meaning as "transcendent," though its root is the same. The latter signifies some being or order of beings that is *above* the ordinary levels of limited, created beings, such as God, whereas "transcendental" signifies in a sense the opposite, that which is found in *every* being. The modern Kantian meaning of this term is quite different again, signifying the necessary a priori conditions of possibility of all human knowing—an epistemological, not an ontological, meaning, typical of a modern philosophical approach.

The significance of identifying and calling attention to these transcendental properties of all being is that they signify aspects of being, rooted *in being itself* and not imposed arbitrarily from outside by human knowers, that are so fundamental to, and inseparable from, being that if they are removed or denied, the whole *objective basis* for our most precious human values—truth, goodness, and beauty—collapses, or is referred back to the fragile, unstable "ground" of our own a priori human subjectivity imposing these values from without, as we see happening in the Kantian and post-Kantian traditions of modern philosophy. It is a most illuminating lesson in the history of philosophy as to how the implications of a philosophical idea slowly work themselves out, when we note that once Kant broke the intrinsic link between being and intelligibility, by holding that beings in themselves are unknown to us but that we impose intelligibility upon them from without, from our own a priori forms of thought, the links between being and the other transcendentals—unity, goodness, and beauty—began to dissolve, one by one: first, the intrinsic *unity* of real beings, which we now impose on them from without; then *goodness,* which, since the intelligibility of things in themselves is unknown to us, must also be imposed by us, either arbitrarily or from some realm of values floating somewhere outside the realm of real being; and finally *beauty,* the beauty of natural things, sundered from being itself as no longer unified, intelligible, or good in itself, must also be imposed by us entirely from within our own subjectivity, either arbitrarily ("Beauty is in the eye of the beholder"), or from some realm of values declared "objective," but floating somewhere independent of real (actually existing) being. The beauty of works of art, it should be added, is a considerably more complicated problem, depending more on human subjectivity, both individual and cultural, but still with *some* rooting in the reality of the work of art in itself—which is itself a unique synthesis of real and mental being, the subjective and the objective. St. Thomas himself does not draw out all these implications in the brief texts selected here; but he lays the indispensable groundwork for them.

Since no commentary on the texts is included here, it will be up to the instructor to fill in the relevant background for interpreting the meaning and significance of the texts themselves. Since the first reading, "On the Division of Speculative Science," is a long and rather technical one, presupposing some familiarity with the curriculum of study in St. Thomas's own day, no longer current in our own, I *suggest* that for beginning students it might be wiser to skip it and begin with Chapter II, Section 1: "On Being as Being," then proceed to Chapter 1, Section 2: "On the Nature of Metaphysics," and then to the other texts in order.

W. Norris Clarke, S.J.
Fordham University, 1997

Some Suggested Introductory Readings

Josef Pieper, *Guide to St. Thomas Aquinas* (Univ. of Notre Dame Press, 1987): best brief guide to his setting and spirit.

Jean-Pierre Torrell, O.P., *St. Thomas Aquinas* (Washington: Catholic Univ. of America Press, 1996), Vol. I: *The Person and His Work:* the best recent scholarly introduction.

Etienne Gilson, *The Christian Philosophy of St. Thomas Aquinas* 5th ed. (New York: Random House, 1956), esp. the new Chapter I: Existence and Reality, on Aquinas's "existentialism."

W. Norris Clarke, S.J., "Action as the Self-Revelation of Being: A Central Theme in the Thought of St. Thomas," Chapter 3 in *Explorations in Metaphysics: Being–God–Person* (University of Notre Dame Press, 1994): texts with commentary on key theme of being as active, to go with the Preface to this book.

PREFACE

THIS BOOK consists of texts from various writings of St. Thomas Aquinas dealing with some major problems of the philosophy of common or universal being; they do not constitute a preface to the whole of metaphysics as conceived by St. Thomas, since, for him, metaphysics is at once first philosophy, so far as it considers the highest causes, and natural theology inasmuch as it considers God; indeed, according to the Angelic Doctor metaphysics in its entirety is ordered to the knowledge of God; because being is first of all God, apart from Whom no being whatever exists.

It is frequently said that metaphysics is the science of being in general. This characterization can be, and sometimes has been, disastrously misleading. Metaphysics is a common science inasmuch as it considers being as common to all that is or can be, but it is not general if this term is taken to imply that its subject (being) and its principles are generic, and therefore univocal, universals. On the contrary, being and its essential properties and divisions are for St. Thomas transcendental principles common analogically or proportionally to all that in any way is. It is hoped that this point may emerge from an attentive reading of the texts.

I trust that sufficient material has been included, particularly in the last two chapters, to make it clear that for St. Thomas metaphysics is primarily and principally about God. The selections that comprise this book, however, aim only at representing some of the chief principles and doctrines of St. Thomas' metaphysics, viewed more especially as *scientia communis* than as first philosophy or as natural theology. Current pedagogical necessities or conditions seem to dictate this preponderantly general-metaphysical collection of Thomistic texts. (An adequate English text, say, for a one-term or half-year course in St. Thomas' self-authored "general metaphysics" is non-existent, whereas a magnificent treatise on natural theology is included within the first twenty-odd Questions of the *Summa Theologica*.) In a word, this little INTRODUCTION is designed to initiate the college or university student, or any interested person, into the so-called general-metaphysical, rather than the natural-theological, part of St. Thomas' integral philosophy of being.

It would be absurd to suppose that this or any translation of St. Thomas can be a wholly adequate substitute for the Latin text itself. Almost every translation is to some extent an interpretation, and perhaps this is particularly true in regard to translations of the great thought-laden writings of the past. I am only claiming that these renderings of the ancient Thomistic texts succeed in conveying the thought of their author with a reasonable degree of accuracy.[1] Hence, while it is perfectly true that studying such a translation is by no means the same thing as studying St. Thomas in his own tongue, it is a fairly close approximation to doing just that.

Now it is often said, and not without considerable truth, that non-professionals, or newcomers to philosophy, cannot really read St. Thomas. But, as every experienced teacher of St. Thomas knows, such persons are often in no better case as regards works about St. Thomas. Indeed, those inexperienced in philosophy (and who does not in some measure or respect fall in that class?) cannot without help from teachers successfully read any truly valuable metaphysics book, Thomist or other. It is of course impossible to comprehend the full contextual significance of the words one sees if one is not a master, if one does not possess in a very

---

1. Although I have consulted various English translations of parts of this collection and found some of them very helpful, I assume complete responsibility for all my translations in this volume. In every case my renderings are based upon the Latin texts of St. Thomas in the best editions immediately available to me.

high and intense degree that firm quality or perfection of mind (that *habitus,* to use the proper technical word for it) which alone makes wisdom attainable. Nevertheless he who, though not in the full sense a master, does enjoy a metaphysical habitus is needed to read the book with those less experienced, that something of the thought of the author might be mediated to them. In principle, there ought to be more chance of significant mediation if this author is himself a master in the eminent sense of the word. Herein lies the chief pedagogical argument for the use of "great books."

Aside from the short treatise *On Being and Essence* (and a few other brief writings on particular metaphysical problems) there exists no "great book" of St. Thomas' own metaphysics. And this little work, one of the Angelic Doctor's earliest, far from seeking to survey the field of "general metaphysics," is, as St. Thomas explains in his own preface to it, concerned only with three specific problems, being largely devoted to the question of the relation of metaphysical principles to logical concepts. As for the Commentary on the *Metaphysics* of Aristotle, St. Thomas does not in it, except rarely (and even then it seems quite incidentally), speak in his own name.[2] One will not find in this voluminous commentary a systematic statement of the distinctive metaphysics which the Angelic Doctor himself developed—not only with the aid of Aristotle, but also of St. Augustine, St. John Damascene, the Pseudo-Dionysius, Boethius, Cicero, Avicenna, Averoes, of many other philosophers and theologians and sages, pagan and Christian, and above all, of

---

2. I do not mean to imply that St. Thomas' commentaries do not represent his true thought. I am only referring to the broad fact that in his Aristotelian commentaries, St Thomas is above all the expositor, while in his theological commentaries, he is above all the mediator; so that, whereas in the first he is almost exclusively concerned with giving a clear account of the essential meaning or intention of the Philosopher's thought, in the second he allows himself a much freer hand. For usually it is in systematizing and drawing out the implications of the theological writings of others that the Angelic Doctor presents and develops his own original metaphysical insights.

Holy Writ. One must then look for this metaphysics throughout the writings of St. Thomas, and one finds it embedded, so to speak, in everything he wrote, but most conspicuously present, perhaps, in some of the Disputed Questions (a prime example is that of the *De Veritate),* and in the two Summae.

Thus, with a view primarily to the needs of students, young or old, and teachers of metaphysics, this compilation of texts is intended simply to present a fair sampling of the wisdom of St. Thomas Aquinas at work upon some perennial problems of the science of being as being and those things that essentially follow upon it.

The advantages for philosophic teaching and learning of a compendium like this merit emphasis. First and foremost is the intellectual challenge offered to teacher as well as student. Both are here confronted pretty directly with the signified thought of a pre-eminent philosophical master. Such a confrontation can be more stimulating and fruitful, in the long run if not immediately, than with any Thomistic commentary, however excellent, however useful or even indispensable. For although not all philosophers are greater than their best commentators, most of them are, and this is indubitably true of St. Thomas.

Moreover, texts of a principal author leave the teacher free to supply his own commentary (unencumbered, perhaps unembarrassed, by the remarks of others), while obliging him to think out a fresh one. This freedom, and the obligation it entails, could prove a great pedagogic boon. Notoriously, the second-rate philosophy manual all too often becomes, for teacher and student alike, a substitute for personal intellectual effort, a soporific instead of a stimulant.

Since it is axiomatic that the teaching of philosophy is genuinely effective only so long as the teacher himself is actually learning, is it not obviously desirable to have a *master* as principal guide and companion in the teacher's own philosophizing and in that of his students? That the kind of cooperative teaching and learning I have in mind can be carried out successfully with the intelligent American undergraduate has been the repeated experience of those who have really tried it. The writings of great philosophers have a kind of natural fitness to awaken and nourish the intellects of beginners as well as of mature thinkers. I do not for a moment intend to suggest that such writings are of value to every category of "beginners." Nor do I condemn the use of doctrinally sound and solid textbooks, however uninspiring. On the contrary, it is evident, I think, that for certain normal and necessary educational ends (e.g., a certain systematic acquaintance with the outlines of the main problems and principles, their location in the various philosophical sciences, and the relationships of these sciences to each other) good commentaries, summaries, digests, in a word, manuals or textbooks, are indispensable, fulfilling as they do the role of maps for travelers in unknown lands.

Concerning the contents of the book itself a few remarks may be useful. First, it will be noted that several important parts of the book, e.g., the sections on the meaning of being and on analogy, are quite brief, even sketchy. They are so of necessity, owing to the paucity of purely metaphysical texts in St. Thomas on these matters. These, and other, sections call for considerable commentary on the part of the professor; so indeed does the book as a whole, and this "privation," so far as it elicits independent effort, quickens and inspires personal thought and reflection, will be a positive educational blessing. Secondly, it is quite possible that this or that professor or discussion leader may not wish, or think it feasible, to attempt to cover in class or meeting all the matter in this collection while others might wish to add, or substitute, a consideration of such topics as the metaphysics of substantial or accidental being, or of the causes of being. But in any case this volume is put forth with the not immoderate claim (so it seems to its compiler and translator) of representing the minimum requirements for a course or plan of study whose object is a rather direct and intimate appreciation of the metaphysical thought of St. Thomas Aquinas in some of its fundamentals.

I wish to thank Mr. Donald A. O'Grady, my graduate assistant, and teaching fellow in philosophy at this university, for his invaluable technical help in preparing the manuscript for publication.

Chapter VI, and section 3 of Chapters VIII and X are printed with the kind permission of Random House, Inc., being taken, for the most part, from *Basic Writings of St. Thomas Aquinas,* edited by A. C. Pegis.

JAMES F. ANDERSON
Department of Philosophy
University of Notre Dame

I

WHAT IS METAPHYSICS?

1. On The Division of Speculative Science[1]

O BJECTIONS. 1. It seems that speculative science is not suitably divided into the three parts: natural science, mathematical science, and divine science. For the parts of speculative science are those firmly and freely established dispositions *(habitus)*[2] which perfect the contemplative part of the soul. But the Philosopher in the sixth book of the *Ethics*[3] states that the scientific part of the soul, which is the contemplative part of it, is perfected by three such dispositions, namely, wisdom, science, and understanding. Therefore the parts of speculative science are these three and not the three aforenamed.

---

1. Commentary on *The Trinity* of Boethius, quest. 5, art. I (*In Boeth. de Trin.*, V, I: "Whether the division is fitting whereby speculative science is divided into these three parts: natural science, mathematical science, and divine science?"). I am indebted to Father Paul Wyser's edition of this work for references to citations made by St. Thomas in this text.

2. There seems to be no single English word that conveys the meaning of *"habitus"*–a meaning radically opposed to that of "habit," as implying a mechanical, unfree, repetitiousness (a "rut") in man's behavior. *"Habitus,"* on the contrary, designates a stable perfection appertaining principally to the free, spiritual soul and necessary in order to raise it to a higher level or to dispose it for and to facilitate operations chiefly of a rational, free, nature, or those under reason's control or command.

3. Cf. *Eth. Nicom.*, VI, 1 (1139a 12 ff.).

2. Augustine says in the eighth book of *The City of God*[4] that rational philosophy, namely, logic, is contained under contemplative or speculative philosophy. Therefore the proposed division, since it makes no mention of logic, seems to be inadequate.

3. Philosophy is commonly divided into the seven liberal arts, among which neither natural philosophy nor divine science is included, but only rational philosophy [logic] and mathematics. Therefore natural philosophy and divine science ought not to be reckoned as parts of speculative science.

4. The science of medicine seems to be especially operative, yet in it one part is deemed speculative and another practical. So likewise, in all other operative sciences there exists a speculative part. Hence in this division mention ought to be made of ethics or moral philosophy, regardless of the fact that it concerns action, on account of the part of it which is speculative.

5. The science of medicine is a certain part of physics [or natural philosophy] and there are other arts that are called mechanical, as the science of agriculture, alchemy, and the like. Because these are operative sciences, it does not seem that natural philosophy ought to be classed without qualification under speculative science.

6. The whole should not be divided in opposition to any of its parts. But divine science seems to be a whole in relation to physics and mathematics, since the subjects of the latter sciences are parts of the subject of divine science. For the subject of divine science, which is first philosophy, is being, of which a part is mobile substance, which natural philosophy considers, and another part quantity, which mathematics studies, as is clear from the third book of the *Metaphysics*[5] Consequently divine science ought not to be divided in opposition to natural philosophy and mathematics.

4. *De Civ. Dei,* VIII, 4 (PL 41, 228; i.e., *Patrologia Latina,* Migne ed., vol. 41, col. 228).

5. Aristotle, *Metaph.,* III (B), 2 (996b 14–23).

7. Sciences are divided as things are divided, as Aristotle points out in the third book of *The Soul.*[6] But philosophy is about being, for it is the knowledge of being, as Dionysius says in his *Letter to Polycarp.*[7] Now it is by the one and the many, by substance and accident, that being is first of all divided in accordance with its [ultimate and all-inclusive] division into potency and act; and thus it seems that the parts of philosophy ought to be distinguished in the same manner.

8. There are many other divisions of beings concerning which there are sciences more essential than those proceeding in accordance with the divisions into the mobile and the immobile, the abstract and the non-abstract. For example, there are the divisions into the corporeal and the incorporeal, the animate and the inanimate, and others of like nature. Therefore the division of the parts of philosophy should be made on the basis of differentiating factors of the latter sort, rather than through those proposed here.

9. That science upon which other sciences are based ought to be prior to them. But all other sciences depend upon the divine science as their foundation, because it belongs to it to prove the principles of the other sciences. Accordingly, divine science ought to be put in its proper order, before the others.

10. That mathematics is prior to natural philosophy in the order of learning is evidenced by the fact that children are able to learn mathematics easily, but not natural philosophy, which can be learned only by those advanced in age [or experience], as Aristotle states in the sixth book of the *Ethics.*[8] Hence, in the sciences the order of learning adhered to by the ancients is said to have been this: first, logic, then mathematics, thirdly natural philosophy, after that moral philosophy, and finally divine science. Therefore mathemat-

6. *De An.,* III, 8 (431b 24).

7. Pseudo-Dionysius, *Epistula* VII, 2 (PG 3, 1080b; i.e., *Patrologia Graeca,* Migne ed., vol. 3, col. 1080b).

8. *Eth. Nicom.,* VI, 9 (1142a 11–19).

ics ought to come before natural science [or philosophy of nature]. The division proposed thus appears inadequate.

On the contrary, the adequacy of this division is proved by the Philosopher in the sixth book of the *Metaphysics* where he says that there will be three parts of philosophical and theoretical science, namely, mathematics, physics [philosophy of nature], and [natural] theology.[9]

Moreover, in the second book of the *Physics*[10] three modes of scientific knowledge are distinguished, and these evidently pertain to the aforesaid division into the three philosophical and theoretical sciences.

Further, in the beginning of the *Almagest*[11] Ptolemy also makes use of the same division.

I answer: It must be said that the theoretical or speculative intellect is distinguished properly from the operative or practical intellect in this: the speculative intellect has for its end the truth which it considers, whereas the practical intellect orders the truth reflected upon to an operation as to its end. For this reason the Philosopher says in the third book of *The Soul* that the speculative and the practical intellect differ from each other in their end;[12] and in the second book of the *Metaphysics* it is said that the end of speculative science is truth, whereas the end of operative science is action.[13] Naturally the subject-matter must be congruent with the end; consequently the subject-matter of the practical sciences must be those things which can be made or done by our work, so that knowledge of them can be ordered to operation as to an end. But the subject-matter of the speculative sciences must be things that are not made by our own work. Therefore the contemplation of such things cannot be ordered to operation as to an end. And it is according to differenti-

9. *Metaph.*, VI (E), 1 (1026a 18).
10. *Phys.*, II, 2 (193b 23; 194b 14).
11. Claudius Ptolemaeus, Syntaxis Mathematica, I, 1 (*Opera Omnia*, I, 5, 7–10).
12. *De An.*, III, 10 (433a 14).
13. *Metaph.*, II (a), 1 (993b 20).

ations found within this order of things that the speculative sciences have to be distinguished.

It must be borne in mind, however, that while habitus or powers are distinguished by objects, they are not distinguished by just any kind of difference at all in these objects. They are distinguished, rather, in accordance with those differentiating characters that essentially belong to their objects precisely as objects. Thus it is merely accidental to the sensible as such that it be an animal or a plant. It is not, then, on any such accidental ground that the senses are distinguished, but rather on the basis of color and sound.[14] Therefore the speculative sciences must be divided according to differences of speculable objects, precisely as such.

Now for that speculable entity which is the object of a speculative power, something is required on the part of the intellective power and something on the part of the habitus of science whereby the intellect is perfected. On the part of the intellect it is required that the object be immaterial, because the intellect itself is also immaterial; as regards the habitus of science, the object must be necessary, because science is of necessary things, as is proved in the first book of the *Posterior Analytics*.[15] Every necessary thing, as such, is immobile, since whatever is moved, so far as it is moved, can be and not be, either in an absolute or in a qualified sense, as is said in the ninth book of the *Metaphysics*.[16] Consequently, separation from matter and motion, and relationship to them, is essential to that speculable entity which is the object of speculative science. Hence it is according to the order of abstraction from matter and motion that the speculative sciences are distinguished.

There are certain objects of speculative knowledge which depend upon matter existentially because they cannot exist except in matter. These are distinguished as follows. Some of them depend upon

14. Which are essential differences of the sensible as such.
15. Aristotle, *Anal. Post.*, 1, 6 (74b 5–75a 17).
16. Aristotle, *Metaph.*, IX Q, 8 (1050b 11-15).

matter both for their being and their being known, such as things in whose definition sensible matter is included, so that they cannot be understood without such matter. In the definition of man, for example, it is necessary to include flesh and bones. It is of such things that physics or natural science treats.[17] But certain other things, though dependent upon matter for their existence, do not so depend for their being known, because in definitions of them sensible matter is not included. Such is the case with lines and number. And of such things mathematics treats.[18] There are still other objects of speculative knowledge, however, which do not depend on matter for existence because they can exist without matter: either they are never found in matter, as God and the angels, or they are in some cases in matter and in other cases not, as substance, quality, being, potency, act, one and many, and things of this sort.[19] The science that treats of all such things is [natural] theology, that is, divine science, its pre-eminent object being God. By another name this science is called metaphysics, that is to say, trans-physics, because it is properly to be learned by us after physics [or natural philosophy], for it is from sensible things that we must take our point of departure in order to arrive at the knowledge of non-sensible things. This science is also called first philosophy, inasmuch as all the other sciences, receiving their principles from it, follow after it. Now, it is impossible that there should be things which depend upon matter for their being known but not for their existence. For the intellect, considered in itself, is immaterial. Consequently there is no fourth generic division of philosophy in addition to the aforenamed three.

Answers to objections. 1. The Philosopher, in the sixth book of the *Ethics*,[20] deals with the intellectual habitus inasmuch as they are intellectual virtues. And they are called virtues so far as they perfect

17. St. Thomas has now defined "the first order" or "degree" of abstraction.
18. This is the second order of abstraction.
19. Namely, all beings not necessarily limited in their realization to the physical or hylomorphic order. This, of course, is the third order of abstraction.
20 *Eth. Nicom.*, VI, 3 ff. (1139b 14 ff).

the intellect in its operation, for a virtue is that which makes its possessor good and his work good. Hence, according as the intellect is perfected in diverse ways by means of diverse speculative habitus of this sort, so are its virtues diversified. One way in which the speculative part of the soul is perfected by the intellect is by the habitus of principles, whereby certain things are known self-evidently. It is perfected in another way when conclusions are known as demonstrated from first principles, whether the demonstration proceeds from lower causes, as in science, or from the highest causes, as in wisdom. Since sciences are distinguished precisely as habitus, they must be differentiated by their objects, that is, by the realities of which they treat. And in such wise are the three parts of speculative philosophy distinguished here and in the sixth book of the *Metaphysics*.[21]

2. As Aristotle makes clear in the beginning of the *Metaphysics*[22] the speculative sciences treat of those things the knowledge of which is sought for its own sake. The objects logic deals with, however, are not inquired into that they may be known for their own sake, but they are sought as a certain aid to the other sciences. For this reason logic is not classed under speculative philosophy as one of its principal parts, but as something reduced, so to say, to speculative philosophy, inasmuch as it provides speculation with its instruments—syllogisms, definitions and other such tools—which we need in the speculative sciences. Thus, as Boethius also observes in his *Commentary on Porphyry*,[23] logic is not so much a science as an instrument of science.

3. The seven liberal arts do not provide an adequate division of theoretical philosophy. Rather, as Hugh of St. Victor says in the third book of his *Didascalon*,[24] the seven liberal arts . . . are classed

21. *Metaph.*, VI (E), 1 (1026a 18).
22. *Metaph.*, I (A), 1 (981b 21, 982a 1); 2 (982a 14-17, 30 f.).
23. *In Isagogen Porphyrii Comm.*, ed. secundae, liber I, cap. 3.
24. Hugo a S. Victore, *Didascalion III,* 3 (PL 176, 768).

with the theoretical sciences simply because it was by them that those who wished to learn philosophy were first instructed. These arts were distinguished into a group of three called the *trivium* and a group of four called the *quadrivium*, so that (as Hugh says) "by them, as by certain roads, the keen mind might enter into the secrets of wisdom." This pedagogical development is quite in accord with what the Philosopher lays down in the second book of the *Metaphysics*, namely, that the method of science ought to be sought before the sciences themselves.[25] The Commentator also, remarking upon the same text,[26] says that, before all the other sciences, one ought to learn logic, which teaches the manner of proceeding in all the sciences. And to logic the *trivium* pertains. Further, in the sixth book of the *Ethics*, the Philosopher says that mathematics can be learned by children, but not physics, which requires experience.[27] Thus are we given to understand that logic ought to be learned first, and then mathematics, to which the *quadrivium* pertains, so that by these pathways, as it were, the soul is prepared for philosophical disciplines of another nature. Now, among the other sciences, logic and mathematics are called "arts," for not only are they cognitive but they also issue in a certain work, which is immediately that of reason itself, such as the orderly arranging of thoughts, forming syllogisms, regulating speech; or [in mathematics] numbering, measuring, constructing [the mathematical bases of] musical harmonies, and computing the course of the stars. Other sciences, however, either are not ordered to making but only to knowledge— as are divine science and the science of nature, which cannot claim the name of art, because art is productive reason, as is said in the sixth book of the *Metaphysics*[28]—, or the sciences besides logic and mathematics are concerned with some corporeal work, as are medicine, alchemy and the like. Hence they cannot be called liberal arts,

25. Cf. *Metaph.*, II (a), 3 (995a 12-14).
26. Averroes, *In II Metaphysicae*, com. 15 (Venetiis 1574, X, fol. 35ʳ).
27. *Eth. Nicom.*, VI, 9 (1142a 11-19).
28. *Metaph.*, VI (E), 1 (1025b 22).

because in them man is engaged in operations belonging to that part of him wherein he is not free, namely, his body. But although moral science is ordered to operation, that operation is not the act of science but of virtue, as is clear from what is said in the *Ethics*.[29] Moral science, therefore, cannot be called an art; rather, in moral operations virtue assumes the role of art. Thus the ancients defined virtue as the art of living well and righteously, as Augustine remarks in the fourth book of *The City of God*.[30]

4. As Avicenna states in the beginning of his book on *Medicine*,[31] the "theoretical" and the "practical" are distinguished in one way when philosophy is divided into theoretical and practical, in another way when the arts are divided into theoretical and practical, and in still another way when medicine is so divided. For when philosophy and even the arts are distinguished as theoretical and practical, this distinction must be taken in reference to their finality, so that what is ordered solely to the knowledge of truth is to be called theoretical, whereas that which is ordered to operation is called practical. However, when philosophy as a whole and the arts are thus classified, it is important that in the division of philosophical science reference be made to man's last end, namely, beatitude, to which the whole of human life is ordered. For, as Augustine says in *The City of God*,[32] quoting Varro,[33] "There is no reason why man should philosophize except that thereby he may be happy." So it is that a twofold felicity is claimed by philosophers: the one contemplative, the other active, as is pointed out in the tenth book of the *Ethics*.[34] And correspondingly they distinguish two parts of philosophy, calling moral philosophy "practical," natural and rational philosophy [i.e., philosophy of nature and logic] "theoretical."

---

29. Cf. Aristotle, *Eth. Nicom.*, VI, 13 (1144b 17-30).
30. *De civ. Dei,* IV, 21 (PL 41, 128; cf. PL 41, 258, 789).
31. *Liber Canonis in Medicina* (Venetiis 1564, I 6).
32. *De civ. Dei*, IX, 1 (PL 41, 623).
33. T. M. Varro, *Liber de Philosophia.*
34. Aristotle, *Eth. Nicom.*, X, 7-8 (1177a 12).

However, when certain arts are said to be "speculative" and others "practical," reference is being made to some special ends of these arts, as when we say that agriculture is a practical art but that dialectics is theoretical. But when medicine is divided into theoretical and practical, it is not with reference to the end of medicine, since if that were the case the whole of medical science would come under the heading of "practical," medicine being [entirely] ordered to operation. The aforesaid division, on the contrary, is made on the grounds of the proximity to or remoteness from operation of the things dealt with in medical science. Thus, that part of medicine is called "practical" which teaches methods of healing; for instance, that in the case of such and such symptoms, such and such remedies are to be applied. But we call "theoretical" that part of medicine which teaches the principles by which the physician is guided in his operation, though not proximately; for example, that the [healing?] powers are three, and how many different kinds of fevers there are. Hence, if a certain part of an operational science is called "theoretical," that part need not be classed under speculative philosophy.

5. One science is contained under another science in two ways: 1) as a part of it, because its subject is a certain part [or type] of natural body, e.g., the science of plants is comprised under natural science as a part; 2) subalternated to it, that is, when in the superior science there is assigned the explanatory cause *(propter quid)* of those things about which, in the lower science, it is known only *that* they are; thus is music, for example, placed under arithmetic. Medicine, then, is not classed under physics as a part of it, since the subject of medicine, as such, is not a part of the subject of natural science. For although the curable body is a natural body, it is not the subject of medicine so far as it is curable by nature, but so far as it is curable by art. But since in the healing which is effected also by art, art is the minister of nature (because some natural power, aided by art, is the cause of healing), the essential explanation *(propter quid)* of the operation which is art must be based upon the properties of natural

things. For this reason medicine is subalternated to physics, and so likewise are alchemy, the science of agriculture, and all other sciences of the same order. It remains, then, that physics in itself and in all its parts is speculative, although some operative sciences are subalternated to it.

6. Although the subjects of the other sciences are parts of being, which is the subject of metaphysics, it does not follow that those sciences are parts of metaphysics. For each science studies a part of being under a special intelligible aspect, distinct from that in which being is contemplated in metaphysics. The subject of such a science is not, properly speaking, a part of the subject of metaphysics, because it is not a part of being in that aspect wherein being is the subject of metaphysics.[35] Rather, in virtue of its own manner of viewing reality, each special science is rendered distinct from every other one. However, a science can be termed a part[36] of metaphysics if it be concerned with potency or act or unity, or anything of the kind,[37] because these principles call for the same mode of consideration as does being, of which metaphysics treats.

7. Those parts [or modes] of being require the same manner of treatment as common being[38] because they also do not depend upon matter. Hence the kind of science that deals with such modes of being does not differ from the science which treats of common being.

8. The various additional divisions of reality which the objection sets forth are not essential differentiating factors of those things considered precisely in so far as they are knowable. Consequently, the sciences are not differentiated by such factors.

9. Although divine science is the first of all sciences, nevertheless for us other sciences are naturally prior. For, as Avicenna says in the beginning of his *Metaphysics*,[39] the position of this science is such that

35. I.e., no science other than metaphysics considers even its own particular subject, *qua* being.
36. Materially speaking.
37. I.e., any transcendental principle.
38. I.e., being as existing actually or possibly in whatever is. This, according to St. Thomas, is the subject of metaphysics.

it is learned after the natural sciences, in which many things are established which this divine science makes use of: generation, for example, corruption, motion, and the like. So, too, it is learned after mathematics. Thus, for theology to acquire knowledge of separated substances, number and the order of the celestial bodies must be known, and knowledge of these things is not possible without astrology, a science to which, in turn, the whole of mathematics is prerequisite. Indeed other sciences—music and ethics, for example—contribute to the full development of divine science. Nor, because the same science [natural theology or metaphysics] which supposes those things that are proved in other sciences is the very science that proves the latter's principles, is there a vicious circle here. For the principles which another science, namely, natural philosophy, receives from first philosophy do not prove those things which the first philosopher appropriates from the natural philosopher. On the contrary, such things are proved by different, self-evident, principles. It is because the first philosopher does not prove the principles which he passes on to the natural philosopher by principles he receives from the latter, but by other self-evident principles, that there is no vicious circle in the first philosopher's definitions. Moreover, the sensible effects from which demonstration in natural science or philosophy proceed are more known to us at first. But when through them we have arrived at a knowledge of first causes, from these latter there will be evident to us the essential explanatory cause *(propter quid)* of those effects, proceeding from which, by way of demonstration of the fact *(demonstratio quia)*, the existence of the first causes was established. In this way natural science contributes something to divine science, and yet it is through divine science that the principles of natural science are made known. And for this reason does Boethius place divine science last: it is the ultimate science in the order of human knowing.

39. *Metaph.,* Tract I, 3 (Venetiis 1508, fol. 71ᵇb–71ᵛa).

10. Although natural philosophy comes to be learned after mathematics, since the universal teachings of natural philosophy require experience and time for their understanding, nevertheless natural things, being sensible, are naturally more accessible to our knowledge than mathematical entities, abstracted as these are from sensible matter.

2. ON THE NATURE AND EXCELLENCE OF METAPHYSICS[40]

As the Philosopher teaches in the *Politics*,[41] when a number of things are ordered to a single thing, one of that number must be regulative or directive, and the others regulated or directed. This indeed is evident in the case of the union of the soul and the body, for the soul naturally commands and the body obeys. So too, within the powers of the soul, the irascible and the concupiscible, by a natural ordering, are governed by the reason. Indeed, all sciences and arts are ordained to one thing, namely, the perfection of man, which is his beatitude. Hence, among them that one must be the mistress of all the others which rightly lays claim to the title of wisdom. For it is the office of the wise to order others.

What this science is and what it treats of can be ascertained if one carefully considers how a person is qualified to rule. Now, as the Philosopher says in the work alluded to,[42] just as men powerful in intellect are naturally the rulers and masters of others—whereas men physically robust yet deficient in intellect are naturally servile—, so, that science is by right naturally mistress of the others which is in the

40. Preface to Commentary on Aristotle's *Metaphysics* (*In Metaph. Aristotelis*, Prooemium).
41. I, 5 (1254a).
42. *Ibid.* (1254b).

highest degree intellectual. This science, however, is the one that treats of the most intelligible things.

The latter we can regard in three ways: firstly, from the standpoint of the order of knowing, for those things that are the source of the intellect's attainment of certitude seem to be the more intelligible ones. Thus, since it is from causes that the intellect achieves the certitude of science, the cognition of causes apparently is in the highest degree intellectual. Consequently that science which considers first causes evidently is regulative of the other sciences.

Secondly, the supremely intelligible objects can be considered from the point of view of the intellect's relation to sense knowledge. For, although the latter is the cognition of particulars, intellect seems to differ from it in this, that intellect comprehends universals. Thus, the science which is maximally intellectual is the one which treats of principles supremely universal. Now, these are being and those things [or principles] that follow upon being, as one and many, potency and act. Such principles, however, ought not to remain completely indeterminate,[43] since without them full cognition of things proper to a given genus or species cannot be had. Moreover, since each genus of beings needs these principles for the very knowledge of itself, they would with equal justification be treated in any particular science at all. It follows that principles of this kind are not to be dealt with in any one *particular* science. Therefore the task of dealing with such principles devolves upon that single common science which, being in the highest degree intellectual, is regulative of the other sciences.

Thirdly, the supremely intelligible objects of which we speak can be considered from the standpoint of the intellect's own cognition. Thus, since every thing has intellective power in consequence of its freedom from matter, those things must be pre-eminently intelligible which exist in complete separation from matter. The intelligible

---

43. I.e., not, as it were, altogether unspecified.

object and the intellect must be proportioned to each other, and must be of one genus,[44] since the intellect and the intelligible are in act one. Now, those things are in the highest degree separated from matter which abstract not only from signate matter, "as do natural forms taken universally, of which natural science[45] treats," but which abstract altogether from sensible matter–and not only according to reason, as mathematical objects do, but also in respect to actual existence, as with God and the intelligences. Evidently, therefore, the science that considers these things is supremely intellectual and the chief or mistress of the others.

Now the foregoing threefold consideration belongs by right not to diverse sciences, but to one science. For the separated substances referred to above are the universal and the first causes of actual being. But it pertains to one and the same science to consider the proper causes of a genus and the genus itself. So it is, for instance, that the natural philosopher studies the principles of the natural body. Of necessity, then, it is the task of the selfsame science to consider not only separated substances but also common being,[46] which is the genus of which these substances are the common and universal causes.

From what has been said it is apparent that, although this science[47] considers the three things just mentioned [48] it does not take this one or that, indifferently, as its subject, but only

44. Throughout this text St. Thomas uses *"genus"* in such a broad sense that it is practically equivalent to what is commonly called "order" or "order of being"; and not once does *"genus"* here signify the logical intention of that name. St. Thomas, following Aristotle, proved that being *(ens)* is not a genus in this strict (logical) sense. E.g., cf. I *Metaph.*, 9, 139; III, 8, 433. (All references to this work use the numbering given in the Cathala edition.)

45. In Aristotle and St. Thomas "natural science" *(scientia naturalis)* is synonymous with "natural philosophy" *(philosophia naturalis)*, namely, philosophy of nature, or "cosmology" as it has been more commonly called since the 18th cetury.

46. *Ens commune*—being as common to all that is in any mode.

47. First philosophy, or metaphysics.

48. Viz., God, the intelligences, common being.

common being. The subject of a science is precisely that whose causes and passions we seek to know, not the causes themselves of any genus that is inquired into. It is the knowledge of the causes of a genus which is the *end* of scientific thought. Although the subject of this science is common being, the latter is predicated of entities that are wholly separated from matter, existentially as well as logically. For among things said to be separated existentially and logically are found not only those that never can exist in matter, as God and intellectual substances, but also those that can be without matter, as common being.[49] This however would not be the case if they depended upon matter in their being.

Therefore, in accordance with the aforesaid three things from which the perfection of this science is derived,[50] it receives three names: "divine science" or "theology"[51] inasmuch as it considers the substances in question;[52] "metaphysics" inasmuch as it considers being and the things that follow upon it—for these transphysical principles are discovered in the process of resolution as the more common after the less common—; and "first philosophy" inasmuch as it considers the first causes of things. It is evident, then, what the subject of this science is, and how it is related to other sciences, and how it is named.

---

49. In this work, St. Thomas often uses the terms *ens commune* and *ens inquantum ens* interchangeably. Thus, St. Thomas here seems to be saying only that being, considered precisely as being, need not be material. Cf. *In Boeth. de Trin.*, V, 1, where this point is explained by St. Thomas.

50. Viz., the fact that it considers the supremely intelligible beings, the most universal or common principles, and the first causes.

51. I.e., natural theology.

52. God and the intelligences.

II

THE SUBJECT OF METAPHYSICS

1. On Being as Being[1]

BECAUSE a science ought to investigate not only its proper subject but also the latter's essential attributes,[2] Aristotle says that there exists a science which takes as its subject being precisely as such, and "those things which belong to being in virtue of its own nature," namely, being's essential attributes.

Aristotle here uses the expression "being in so far as it is being" because the other sciences, which treat of particular beings, do indeed consider being, for all the subjects of sciences are beings, yet they do not consider being as being, but as this sort of being; for example, number, line, fire, or something of the kind.

Aristotle employs the phrase "and those things belonging to being in virtue of its own nature," not simply "those things which appertain to or exist in being," in order to point out that it is not the office of a science to consider those things that exist in its subject accidentally but only those that are present in it essentially. Thus, geometry is not concerned with the question whether a triangle is made of copper or of wood, but only with its absolute nature, according to which it has three equal angles.[3] It does not, therefore, appertain to the science whose subject is being to consider all that exists in it accidentally,

1. The following five paragraphs are taken from the Commentary on Aristotle's *Metaphysics*, Book IV, lect. 1 (*IV Metaph.*, 1, 529-32).
2. The inseparable accidents appertaining to that subject as such.
3. Geometry deals only with the essential properties of its objects.

since it would then be taking into account accidents which are investigated in all sciences. For although all accidents exist in some being, not all accidents exist in a being inasmuch as it is being. Thus essential accidents of an inferior or a subordinate thing are accidental accidents in relation to the superior; for example, accidents essential to man are not essential to animal.[4]

The necessity of this science of metaphysics, which contemplates being and its essential attributes, is manifest; such things ought not to remain unknown because it is upon them that knowledgeof other things depends, for on the knowledge of common or universal things hinges the knowledge of proper or individual things.

That this science is not a particular science, Aristotle shows by the following argument. No particular science considers universal being as such, but only some part of being cut off from its other parts, and of this separated part it examines the essential attribute. The mathematical sciences, for instance, investigate a particular kind of being, namely, the quantitative,[5] whereas the common science, metaphysics, considers universal being as being. Therefore it is not to be identified with any particular science.

No particular science treats of being as being, that is, being-in-common, nor does any particular science treat of any particular being, simply as being. For instance, arithmetic does not consider number as being, but as number. It is the office of the metaphysician, however, to consider any and every being, precisely as being.[6]

---

4. E.g., risibility, the capacity for laughter, is an essential accident—an inseparable property or attribute—of man, but in relation to animal nature as such it is, so to speak, only an accidental accident.

5. Thus mathematics, like all the particular sciences, treats of some essential mode of being; it takes a "part" of being and considers it under that aspect or attribute that belongs to it essentially.

6. VI Metaph., 1, 1147. It is for this reason that metaphysics is called the universal science, or the common science. Logic is equally as universal in its scope as metaphysics, for "all beings fall under the consideration of reason" (IV Metaph., 4, 574). But logic and metaphysics differ primarily in this, that while it pertains to meta-

And because it pertains to the same science to consider being as being, "and, concerning being, what it is," namely, its essence (for every thing has actual existence through its essence), so it is that the particular sciences . . . are not concerned with the problem of determining what being is—its quiddity or essence and its definition, which signifies the essence. Rather, from the essence such sciences proceed to other matters, using the presupposed essence, as if it were an already demonstrated principle, in order to prove other things.[7]

Just as no particular science determines the essence of its subject, so none of them says regarding its subject, that it is or is not. And understandably so; for it belongs to one and the same science to settle the problem of existence and to discover the essence. . . . It is proper to the philosopher, to him who studies being as being, to consider both problems. But every particular science presupposes concerning its own subject both that it is and what it is, as Aristotle states in the first book of the *Posterior Analytics*. And this shows that no particular science treats of being as such, nor of any being precisely as being.[8]

2. THE MEANING OF BEING *(ens)*

A. In Relation to the Act of Existing *(esse)*

That which first falls under the intellect's grasp is being *(ens)*. Thus the intellect necessarily attributes being to everything it apprehends.[9] *Being* means that-which-is, or exists *(esse habens)*.[10]

physics to consider every and any being, precisely as existing, actually or possibly, it is the office of logic to treat of any and every being, precisely as known or as knowable, i.e., as existing in the reason actually or possibly.

7. *Ibid.*, n. 1148.

8. *Ibid.*, n. 1151.

9. Disputed *Questions On Truth*, quest. 21, art. 4, reply to 4th obj. (*De Ver.*, XXI, 4, ad 4).

10. *XII Metaph.*, 1, 2419.

The verb *is consignifies* composition,[11] because it does not signify this principally but secondarily. *Is* signifies primarily that which the intellect apprehends as being absolutely actual, for in the absolute sense *is* means to be in act, and thus its mode of signification is that of a verb. But, since the actuality which *is* principally signifies is universally the actuality of every form, whether substantial or accidental, when we wish to signify that any form or any act whatever actually exists in a subject, we express that fact by this verb *is*.[12]

The word *being (ens)* is imposed from the very act of existing, as Avicenna remarks, whereas the word *thing (res)* is imposed from the essence or quiddity.[13] *Being* properly signifies: something-existing-in-act.[14] *Being* means that-which-has-existence-in-act. Now, this is substance, which subsists.[15]

The act of existing *(esse)* is that by which substance is given the name of being *(ens)*.[16] This act is the actuality of every form or nature.[17]

What[18] I call *esse* is among all principles the most perfect; which is evident from the fact that act is always more perfect than potentiality.[19] Now, any designated form is understood to exist actually only in virtue of the fact that it is held to *be*. Thus, humanity or fire can be considered as existing in the potentiality of matter, or as

---

11. Viz., the composition of predicate with subject in the judgment.

12. Commentary on Aristotle's work *On Interpretation,* Book I, lect. 5, end (I *Peri Hermeneias,* 5, fin.).

13. Commentary on Peter Lombard's *Sentences,* Book I, distinction 8, quest. 1, art. 1 (*I Sent.,* VIII, 1, 1).

14. *Summa Theologica,* First Part, quest. 5, art. 1, reply to 1st obj. (*ST* 1, 5, 1, ad 1).

15. *XII Metaph.,* 1, 2419.

16. *Summa Contra Gentiles,* Book II, chap. 54 (*CG* II, 54).

17. *ST* I, 3, 4.

18. The following two paragraphs are taken from the Disputed Questions *On the Power of God,* quest. 7, art. 2, reply to 9th obj. (*De Pot.,* VII, 2, ad 9). Cf. *ST* I, 4, 1, ad 3.

19. Potentiality basically and primarily means capacity for being-in-act-for *esse*.

existing in the active power of an agent, or also as existing in an intellect. But that which has *esse* is made actually existent. It is evident, therefore, that what I call *esse* is the actuality of all acts, and for this reason it is the perfection of all perfections. Nor is it to be thought that something is added to what I call *esse* which is more formal than *esse* itself, thus determining it as an act determines a potentiality. For the *esse* I speak of is essentially other than that to which it is added as a certain determining principle.[20]

Now, nothing can be added to *esse* that is extraneous to it, since nothing is extraneous to it except nothing *(non-ens)*. . . . *Esse,* then, is not determined by another as a potentiality is determined by an act, but *esse* is determined as an act by a potentiality. . . .[21] And in this way is one *esse* distinguished from another *esse,* namely, according as it is the *esse* of this nature, or essence, or of that.

Esse is what is innermost in each and every thing, and what is deepest in them all, for it is formal in respect of all that is in a thing.[22]

Esse itself is act in relation to both composite and simple natures. Composite natures are not made specifically what they are by this act, but rather by the form in them, for specification concerns a thing's essence whereas *esse* evidently pertains to the question whether a thing is. Nor are angelic substances so specified. Rather, their differentiation into species is based on those simple subsisting forms which they themselves are, and which differ specifically according to their own grade of perfection.[23]

Taken absolutely, as including in itself every perfection of being, *esse* is superior to life and to all other subsequent perfections. . . .

---

20. The act of existing is essentially diverse from the essence which it actualizes or determines to be.

21. The basic "potentiality" that determines *esse* is the essence.

22. *ST* I, 8, 1.

23. Disputed Questions *On Spiritual Creatures,* art. 8, reply to 3rd obj. (*De Spiritualibus Creaturis,* VIII, ad 3).

Yet if *esse* is considered as it is participated in any thing whatever which does not possess the total perfection of being, but has imperfect being—and this is the case with all creatures—, then clearly *esse* in union with the superadded perfection is higher. Accordingly Dionysius says that living things are better than merely existing things, and intelligent things than merely living things.[24]

Esse, as such, is nobler than everything that follows upon it.[25] Thus, considered absolutely and in itself, this act is nobler than the act of understanding. . . . Indeed, that which excels in being *(in esse)* is purely and simply nobler than any thing which excels in any perfection consequent upon being. . . .[26]

B. In Relation to Essence

Being *(ens),* understood as signifying the entity of a thing *(entitas rei),* is divided into the ten categories, and thus taken, being *(ens)* is convertible with thing *(res).*[27]

The name *essence* is taken from being expressed in the first mode [namely, as it is divided into the ten categories], not from being expressed in the second mode [namely, as it signifies the truth of propositions]. For, as is clear in the case of privations, in the latter mode we call some things beings which do not have an essence. . . . Because *being* said in the first mode is divided into the ten categories, *essence* must signify something common to all natures, through which di-

---

24. *ST* I-II, 2, 5, ad 2.
25. Viz., all modes of being.
26. *I Sent.,* XVII, 1, 2, ad 3.
27. *ST* I, 48, 2, ad 2. It is crucially important to note that it is being as essence, and not as in act of being, which is distributed among the categories. "Nothing," says St. Thomas *(De Pot.,* VII, 3), "is placed in a category according to its act of existing (esse) but only by reason of its quiddity."

verse beings are placed in diverse genera and species. For instance, humanity is the essence of man, and so with other things.[28]

Moreover,[29] since that by which a thing is constituted in its proper genus and species is what is signified by the definition indicating what the thing is, philosophers have taken to using the name quiddity for the name essence. The Philosopher frequently calls this the *quod quid erat esse:*[30] that by which a thing is a *what.* It is also called form inasmuch as form signifies the complete essential determination[31] of each thing. . . . Also, it is called nature . . . according as nature is said to be that which can be grasped by the intellect in any way; for a thing is intelligible only by its definition and essence. . . . But "nature" also seems to signify the essence of the thing as ordered to its proper operation, for nothing is without its proper operation. The name quiddity, on the other hand, is derived from that which is signified by the definition, whereas essence means that through which and in which a thing has its act of existing.

---

28. *On Being and·Essence,* Ch. I (*De Ente et Essentia,* I).

29. *Ibid.*

30. St. Thomas' literal translation of Aristotle's τὸ τί ἦν εἶναι Post. Anal., I, 22 (82b 38); *De Anima,* III, 6 (430b 28); *Metaph.,* VII, 3 (1028b 34)—, a phrase untranslatable literally into clear English.

31. The meaning of the Avicennian word *"certitudo,"* which St. Thomas uses here, is not conveyed in English by "certitude" or "fixity" or by any such single word. "Form" in this statement signifies the whole essence.

III

MODES AND DIVISIONS OF BEING (ENS)

1. Ways of Predicating "Being"

BEING IS SPOKEN of in many ways. In one way, something is called a being because it subsists in itself;[1] in another way because it is a principle of subsisting being, as in the case of form; thirdly, because it is a disposition of a subsisting being—for instance, a quality; fourthly, because it is a privation of a disposition of a subsisting being, such as blindness.[2]

Being,[3] expressed in one way, is divided into the ten categories, and it then signifies something existing in nature, whether it be a substance, as man, or an accident, as color. In a second mode, being signifies the truth of a proposition, inasmuch as it is said that an affirmation is true when it signifies that that which is, is, and a negation is true when it signifies that that which is not, is not. Being, taken in this sense, signifies the composition which the intellect, composing and dividing, introduces. Thus, all things which are called beings in the first way are beings also in the second way, for everything that has natural being in things can be signified to exist by an affirmative proposition, as when it is said: color is, or man is. But not all those entities that are beings in the second mode are beings also in the first mode. For an affirmative proposition is made

1. I.e., exists substantially.
2. Disputed Questions On Truth, quest. 21, art. 4, reply to 4th obj. (De Ver., XXI, 4, ad 4).
3. The following paragraph is from II Sent., XXXIV, 1, 1.

regarding a privation, such as blindness, when it is said: blindness is. And yet blindness is not a being existing in the nature of things; it is the loss of some actual entity. In a word, even privations and negations are called beings according to the second mode, but not the first. As regards both these modes, however, *being* is predicated in diverse ways. Taken in the first mode, being is a substantial predicate, and pertains to the question, *what* a thing is; in the second mode, being is an accidental predicate . . . and pertains to the question, *whether* a thing is.[4]

Being[5] is not placed in the definition of *creature,* because being is neither a genus nor a difference. Being is participated in as a reality *not* existing *from* the essence of the thing; and for this reason the question, *whether* a thing is, is other than the question, *what* a thing is. Now, inasmuch as everything outside the essence of a thing may be called an "accident,"[6] that *esse* which pertains to the question, whether a thing is, is an "accident." The Commentator [Averroes] thus states . . . that the proposition, "Socrates is," belongs in the class of accidental predication, according as it imports the entity of real being, or the truth of proposition. Yet it is true that, so far as it implies the real subject *(res)* to which this act of existing belongs, the name *being* signifies the essence of such subjects, and is divided into the ten categories—though not univocally, because actual existence does not belong to all things according to the same concept.[7]

Note that *esse* is not an accident generically so called, where *esse* signifies the act of existing of the substance—for this is the act of the essence—, but *esse* is termed an "accident" because of a

---

4. So, St. Thomas continues, taking being in the second mode, we say absolutely that evils *are* in the universe.

5. *Quodlibetal Questions,* quodl. 2, quest. 2, art. 3 *(Quodl.* II, 2, 3).

6. Taking *accidens* with reference only to its participial sense of "acceding to."

7. Because it does not exist in all beings in the same mode.

certain likeness, seeing that this act is not a part of the essence any more than an accident is.[8]

Being[9] is twofold: being-of-reason and being-of-nature. *Being-of-reason* is predicated properly of those intentions which the reason discovers in the things it considers, such as the generic, the specific, and other like intentions—which indeed are not found in the nature of things, but follow upon the consideration of reason. And this kind of being, namely, being-of-reason, is properly the subject of logic. Now, intelligible intentions of the sort spoken of are paralleled by beings-of-nature, since all beings-of-nature come within the purview of reason. The subject of logic thus extends to all the things of which *being-of-nature* is predicated. Aristotle therefore concludes that the subject of logic is paralleled by the subject of philosophy, which is being-of-nature, real being. Hence the philosopher proceeds from the principles of real being itself in order to prove whatever has to be taken into account respecting its common accidents. In the consideration of these matters the dialectician,[10] on the other hand, proceeds from intentions of reason, which are extraneous to the nature of things.

There[11] is, however, a fourfold division of being: into essential being *(ens per se)* and accidental being *(ens per accidens),* into real being, or being-of-nature, and being-of-reason, into the ten categories, and into actual and potential being. Observe that the division of being into essential and accidental is not the same as the

---

8. *De Pot.* V, 4, ad 3. The act of substantial being is called an "accident" only analogically, inasmuch as, like the predicamental accident, it is not included in the essence, but "accedes to" it. This "likeness" must be understood formally; for the predicamental accident, while not a part of the essence strictly and specifically so called, nevertheless is an *essential* determination, whereas *esse* is altogether outside the order of essence.

9. *IV Metaph.,* 4, 574.

10. And thus also, the logician.

11. *V Metaph.,* 9, 885, with 889 f., 897; VI, 2, 1171; and *ST* III, 10, 3. The foregoing is a summary, not a verbatim translation.

division of being into substance and accident. . . . It is by the absolute consideration of being that it is divided into substance and accident; e.g., whiteness, so considered, is called an accident, and man a substance. Accidental being, however, can be grasped [not absolutely or in itself, but] only through the comparison of accident to substance. And this comparison is signified by the verb *is*, e.g.,: the man *is* white; a predication which, taken as a whole, is an instance of accidental being. Thus it is evident that the division of being into essential and accidental arises from the fact that something is *predicated* of a thing either essentially or accidentally. The division of being into substance and accident, on the other hand, results from the fact that a thing *in its nature* is either a substance or an accident.

Accidental being,[12] again, is spoken of in three ways: firstly, when an accident is predicated of an accident—e.g., "the just [man] is musical"; secondly, when an accident is predicated of a subject—e.g., "the man is musical"; thirdly, when a subject is predicated of an accident—"the musical [person] is a man."

Further,[13] respecting the mode of essential being, Aristotle first distinguishes it into the ten categories, pointing out that being in this mode is extramental and is called "perfect" or complete being. Secondly, he notes another mode according to which being exists only in the mind. Thirdly, he divides being into potentiality and act. So divided, being is more common than perfect being, namely, than being as divided into the ten categories. For potential being is being only in a qualified and imperfect sense. Aristotle asserts that those things are said to *be,* in an absolute sense, which signify the categories. Now it must be well understood that being cannot be limited to some determinate entity in the manner in which a genus is limited to species through differences. For the difference, since it

---

12. *Ibid.,* n. 886.
13. *V Metaph.,* 9, 889.

does not participate in the genus,[14] is outside the essence of the genus. But nothing can be outside the essence of being so as to constitute some species of being by addition to being; for what is outside being is nothing. . . . Hence the Philosopher had proved in the third book of his *Metaphysics*[15] that being cannot be a genus.

Therefore[16] being must be limited to diverse genera in accordance with diverse modes of predication—which themselves follow upon diverse modes of existing, because in as many ways as something is predicated, in just so many ways is something signified to *be*. And for this reason those things into which being is first divided are called predicaments, because they are distinguished according to the various modes of predicating.

There[17] are indeed some predications in which the verb *is* does not explicitly occur. Let it not be supposed that in such cases (e.g., in "the man walks") *being* is not predicated. Denying such a false inference, the Philosopher lays it down that in all such predications something is signified *to be*. In fact, every verb is reduced to this verb *is*, and its participial form [be-*ing*]. There is, then, no difference between saying that a man is convalescing and that he convalesces; and so in all other cases. It is therefore evident that in as many modes as predication is made, in just so many ways is being spoken of.

2. The Division of Being by Potency and Act

The primary simple principles cannot be defined, for in definitions there can be no infinite regress. *Act* is such a principle. Therefore it

---

14. Put in logical terms, the concept of the difference is not included in the concept of the genus.

15. *Metaph.*, III (B), 3 (998b 18–26).

16. *V Metaph.*, 9, 890.

17. *Ibid.*, n. 893.

cannot be defined. Yet, through the proportion of two things to each other, it can be seen what act is. So if we take the relation of the builder to the buildable, and of one who is awake to one asleep, and of that which sees to that which has its eyes closed while having the power of sight . . . , proportionally, from such particular examples, we can arrive at a knowledge of what act and potency are.[18]

Potency[19] is spoken of in relation to act. But act is twofold: first act, which is form, and second act, which is operation. As the common understanding of the term indicates, *act* was attributed first of all to action; almost everyone understands *act* to mean this. However, from this meaning the term act was transferred to signify the form, seeing that form is a principle of action, and an end. Potency, then, is likewise twofold: active potency, to which the act that is operation corresponds—and to this the term *potency*[20] seems to have been attributed primarily—and passive potency, to which first act, namely the form, corresponds—and to this the term *potency* was likewise, it seems, attributed secondarily.

Now,[21] in any two things whatever, if one of them completes the other, then the relation between them is that of act to potentiality; for nothing is brought to completion, fulfilled, except by its own act. . . . But it is the act of existing itself which completes, fulfills, the existing substance; each and every being is in act as a result of having the act of existing. It follows that in every one of the aforesaid substances[22] there is a composition of act and potentiality.

Moreover, in a thing that which is derived from an agent must be act; for an agent's office is to make something actual. But it was

18. *IX Metaph.*, 5, 1826 f.

19. *De Pot.*, I, 1.

20. St. Thomas is using the one word, *potentia,* to signify potency in any mode; whereas in English "power" is almost always used to designate active *potentia* alone. Let us use "potentiality" to signify passive *potentia.*

21. The following four paragraphs are found in *CG* II, 53. Cf. *ST* I, 77, 1: Potentiality and act divide every being and every genus of being.

22. I.e., created intellectual ones; but the argument applies to all other created substances as well.

proved earlier that all substances except the first have existence from it. In every case it is because they receive their existence from something else that caused substances themselves *are*. This very existence, then, is present in caused substances as their act. That in which an act is present is a potentiality. Indeed act as such is referred to potentiality. Hence, in every created substance there is potentiality and act.

Again. Whatever participates in something is related to that which is participated as potentiality to act.[23] For, through that which is participated [received] the participator is actualized in such and such a manner. But it was shown previously that God alone is being in virtue of His own essence, while all other things participate in the act of existing.[24] Every created substance therefore, is related to its own existence as potentiality to act.[25]

Further. It is through an act that a thing becomes like its efficient cause; for an agent produces its like so far as it is in act. But every created substance attains likeness to God through the very act of existing *(ipsum esse)*, as was proved earlier. Therefore, existence itself *(ipsum esse)* has this status with respect to all created substances: it is their act. Thus, in every created substance there is composition of act and potentiality.

In[26] every composite being[27] there must be act and potentiality. Indeed no plurality can become one in an absolute sense unless in it something be act and something else potentiality. [Complete]

---

23. The participator is the receiver of the participated and as such is potential with respect to the latter.

24. They exist and are not the existence they have.

25. *As subject* of an existence which it itself is not, every creature is but a certain receptive capacity—a potentiality—for that act *(esse)* which purely and simply makes it to be.

26. *CG* I, 18.

27. And, as we have seen, such is every creature. Cf. *ST* I, 3, 7: "In every composite, there must be potentiality and act . . . , for either one of the parts actualizes

entities actually existing do not form a unit, except, as it were, by way of conjunction or aggregation; and thus united they are not one in an absolute sense. But even in such wholes, the parts themselves are potential with respect to their unification, since they are unified actually after having been unified potentially. . . . Moreover, every composite, precisely as composite, is potentially dissolved, although in certain things something is present that resists dissolution. But what is dissoluble is in potentiality with respect to non-existence.

Every[28] thing other than God has being participatively; so that in it substance [or essence], sharing the act of existence, is other than this act itself which is shared. But every participator is related to that which is participated in it as potentiality to act. Hence, the substance of every created thing whatever is to its own existence as potentiality to act. So it is that every created substance is composed of potentiality and act, or, as Boethius says, of what-it-is *(quod est)* and act of existing *(esse)*.

3. THE REAL COMPOSITION OF ESSENCE AND ACT OF EXISTING

It is clear from what has been said already that in every created thing essence is *distinct* from existence and is compared to the latter as potentiality to act.[29] Every created being participates in the act of existing;[30] God alone is His act of existing.[31] The act of existing of every finite thing is participated, because no thing outside God is its own act of existing.[32]

another, or in any case all the parts are as it were in potency with respect to the constitution of the whole."
28. *Quodl.,* III, 20.
29. *ST* I, 54, 3.
30. Possesses *esse* without being one with it.
31. Cf. *ST* I, 3, 4.
32. *CG* III, 65.

Whatever[33] is participated is related to the participator as its act. . . . But participated act of existing is limited by the [receptive] capacity[34] of the participator. Hence God alone, who is His own act of existing, is pure and infinite act. In intellectual substances, indeed, there is a composition of act and potentiality; not, however, of matter and form, but of form[35] and participated act of existing.

Now,[36] act of existing, as such, cannot be diverse;[37] yet it can be diversified by something extrinsic to itself; for instance, a stone's act of existing is other than that of a man.

God's[38] act of existing is distinguished and set apart from every other act of existing by the fact that it is self-subsistent, and does not come to a nature [or an essence] other than itself. Every other act of existing, being non-subsisting, must be individuated by the nature and substance which subsists in that act of existing. And regarding these things [namely all creatures] it is true to say that the act of existing of this one is other than the act of existing of that one, inasmuch as it belongs to another nature. So, if there were one color existing in itself, without matter, or without a subject, by this very fact it would be distinguished from every other color; since colors existing in subjects are distinguished only through those subjects.

Because[39] the quiddity of an intelligence[40] is that very intelligence itself, its quiddity or essence is that which it itself is, and its existence, received from God, is that by which it subsists in the nature of things. Some therefore have said that substances of this

33. *ST* I, 75, 5, ad 4.
34. I.e., the passive potency, or the potentiality.
35. Which in the angel *is* the essence.
36. *CG* II, 52.
37. And hence cannot be pluralized or multiplied; *esse,* considered in itself, is simply other than essence, whereby alone *esse* can be diversified, and, so to speak, distributed among beings.
38. *De Pot.,* VII, 2, ad 5.
39. *De ente et essentia,* IV (Chapter numbering of the Roland-Gosselin edition).
40. I.e., an angelic spiritual substance.

kind are composed of that-by-which-they-are (the *quo est*) and that-which-they-are (the *quod est*), or of that-by-which-they-are and essence. . . .

Whatever[41] does not belong to the concept of essence or quiddity comes from without and enters into composition with the essence, for no essence can be understood without its essential parts. But every essence or quiddity can be understood without anything being known of its actual existence. For example, I can understand what a man or a phoenix is and yet be ignorant whether either one exists in reality.[42] It is evident, then, that act of existing is other than essence or quiddity—unless, perhaps, there exists a reality whose quiddity is its very act of existing.[43] And there can be only one such reality: the First Being. . . . In every other being, act of existing is other than quiddity, nature, or form.

The[44] act of existing belongs to the first agent, God, through His own nature; for God's act of existing is His substance. . . . But that which belongs to something according to its own nature, appertains to other things only by participation. . . . Thus the act of existing is possessed by other things, from the First Agent, through a certain participation. But that which a thing has by participation is not its very own substance. Therefore it is impossible that the substance of anything except the first agent should be the act of existing itself.

Now,[45] the composition of matter and form is not of the same nature as the composition of substance and act of existing, though both compositions are of potentiality and act. This is so, first of all,

41. *De ente et essentia, ibid.*

42. This illustrates the capital point that knowledge of an essence does not *itself* give or include any knowledge whatever of its existence.

43. This "perhaps" is purely rhetorical and does not indicate any doubt in St. Thomas' mind that such a Being exists; for, as we see, St. Thomas here refers to God—*Ipsum Esse Subsistens.*

44. *CG* II, 52 (near the end of chapter).

45. The concluding five paragraphs are taken from *CG* II, 54.

because matter is not the very substance of a thing. If it were, then all forms would be accidents, as the ancient Naturalists[46] thought. Rather, matter is a part of the substance. Secondly, this is so because the act of existing itself is not the proper act of the matter, but of the whole substance. For *esse* is the act of that whereof we can say: it *is*; *esse* is not said of the matter, but of the whole. Matter, therefore, cannot be termed that-which-is. On the contrary, the substance itself is that-which-is. Thirdly, the aforesaid compositions are diverse, because the form is not the act of existing, though between the two there exists a certain order. Form is compared to the act of existing as light to the act of illuminating, for instance, or as whiteness to the act of being white. Finally, there is this consideration: existence is act even in relation to the form itself. For in things composed of matter and form, the form is said to be a principle of existing because it is what completes the substance, whose act is *esse* itself; just as the air's transparency is the principle of illumination because it makes the air a proper subject [or receiver] of light.

To sum up: in things composed of matter and form, neither the matter nor the form can be designated as that-which-is, nor even can the act of existing be so designated. However, form can be called that-by-which-a-thing-is, or exists, *(quo est),* inasmuch as it is a principle of existing. Nevertheless, it is the whole substance which is that-which-is *(quod est),* and the act of existing is that by which the substance is denominated a *being.*

In intellectual substances (which . . . are not composed of matter and form, but form in them is itself a subsisting substance) form is that-which-is *(quod est),* whereas *esse* is act and that-by-which the form is *(quo est).* So in them there is but one composition of act and potentiality, namely, the composition of substance and act of existing, which by some is called a composition of that-which-is *(quod est)* and act of existing *(esse),* or of that-which-is *(quod est)* and that-by-which-it-is *(quo est).*

---

46. The pre-Socratic philosophers of nature.

On the other hand, in substances composed of matter and form there is a twofold composition of potentiality and act: first, that of the substance itself, which is composed of matter and form; second, that of the substance, thus composed, and its act of existing. This composition also can be called one of that-which-is *(quod est)* and act of existing *(esse)*, or of that-which-is *(quod est)* and that-by-which-it-is *(quo est)*.

It is evident, therefore, that the composition of act and potentiality is more comprehensive than that of form and matter; matter and form divide natural substance, potentiality and act divide universal being. Accordingly, whatever follows upon potentiality and act, as such, is common to both material and immaterial created substances, as *to receive* and *to be received, to perfect* and *to be perfected.* Yet, all that is proper to matter and form, as such, as *to be generated* and *corrupted,* and the like, appertain to material substances only, and in no way belong to immaterial created substances.

IV

THE ANALOGICITY OF BEING

1. Some Primary Considerations

A LL THE things of which one common term is predicated analogically, not univocally, come within the field of one science. Now being *(ens)* is in this manner predicated of all beings. Consequently all beings are embraced in the scope of that single science which treats of being as being.[1]

In predications all univocal terms are reduced to one first non-univocal, analogical term, which is being *(ens)*.[2]

Being *(ens)* is not a genus, but is predictable analogically of all things in general; and the same must be said concerning the other transcendentals.[3]

There is something analogically common to being and non-being[4] because non-being is itself called being analogically, as is clear from the fourth book of Aristotle's *Metaphysics*.[5]

---

1. *IV Metaph.,* 1, 534.
2. *ST* I, 13, 5, ad 1.
3. *On the Nature of the Genus,* near the end *(De natura generis, I, in fine)*. This *Opusculum,* considered authentic by Msgr. Grabmann, is thought to be of doubtful authenticity by Father Mandonnet. In any case it contains a great deal of sound Thomistic doctrine, as exemplified in the text just cited.
4. Though non-being is a mere being-of-reason, having, of course, no basis in reality.
5. Γ, 2 (1033b 10).

Therefore the distance of nature between the creature and God cannot stand in the way of a community of analogy between them.[6]

As the Philosopher says, the term *being,* or *that-which-is,* is used in various senses. It must be borne in mind that a term is predicated of diverse things in several different ways. 1) In some cases the term is predicated according to a concept altogether identical, and then it is said to be predicated univocally, as *animal,* said of the horse and the cow. 2) In other instances the term is predicated according to concepts altogether diverse in meaning, and then it is said to be predicated of things equivocally, as *dog,* said of the animal of that name and of a certain heavenly body. 3) In still other cases the term is predicated according to concepts diverse in some respect and in some respect not—diverse inasmuch as they entail diverse relations, but one in that these diverse relations are all referred to some one term. A thing is then said to be "predicated analogically," that is, proportionally, each member of the analogy being predicated according to its relation to that one term.[7]

Now[8] a term is predicated analogically in three ways: 1) solely as regards the concept involved; 2) as regards the act of existing, but not the concept; 3) as regards both the concept and the act of existing.

The first mode of analogical predication[9] is present when one concept is attributed to a number of things by priority and

---

6. *De Ver.,* II, 11, ad 5. "The unity of metaphysics, and hence its very existence as a science, is made possible only through the reduction of its multiform objects (substance, accident, becoming, the opposites—even non-being) to the analogical unity of being. This reduction can be effected, for, though being is diversely participated in all beings, it nonetheless in some way exists in them all." James F. Anderson, *The Bond of Being* (St. Louis: Herder, 1949), p. 316.

7. *IV Metaph.,* 1, 535.

8. The following four paragraphs, slightly rearranged, are taken from *Comment. in I Sent.,* XIX, 5, 2, ad 1.

9. Commonly referred to as "analogy of proportion or attribution."

posteriority, yet is realized in but one of them. Thus the concept of health is applied to the animal, to urine, and to diet in various ways, according to priority and posteriority, though not according to a diverse act of existing, because health exists actually only in the animal.[10]

The second mode of analogical predication[11] is in effect when several things are put on an equal footing under one and the same common concept, although the nature that they share in common exists diversely in them. Thus all bodies [however diverse they may be in their actual existence] are on a par so far as the concept of corporeity is concerned. Thus the logician, who considers intentions only, says that the term *body* is predicated univocally of all bodies, and yet corporeity does not exist in corruptible and in incorruptible bodies in the same mode. Hence, for the metaphysician and the philosopher of nature, who consider things in their actual being, neither the term *body* nor any other term is said univocally of corruptible and incorruptible things, as is clear from what the Philosopher[12] and the Commentator say.

The third mode of analogical predication[13] is found where there is no equality either with respect to the common concept involved or to actual existence. It is in this mode that being *(ens)*, for instance, is predicated of substance and of accident. And in all such cases[14] the common term must exist in some way in each of the things of which it is predicated, while differing with respect to greater or lesser perfection.[15]

---

10. Note that the concept here is univocal in itself and is only used analogically.
11. Called by Cajetan "analogy of inequality."
12. Cf. Aristotle, *Metaph.,* I (a), 10.
13. Analogy of proper proportionality.
14. Viz., in all instances of proper proportionality.
15. "And so," St. Thomas continues, "I say that truth and goodness and all such terms [i.e., all terms signifying pure perfections] are in this mode predicated analogically of God and creatures."

It[16] happens in two ways that a term is predicated of a number of things according to different concepts. In one way, according to concepts completely diverse, having no relationship to one [common meaning]. And such things are said to be equivocal by chance, because it is only fortuitously that a man applies one name to one thing and another name to something else, as is particularly evident in the case of different men who are called by the same name. In another way, one name is predicated of a number of things according to concepts not totally other but agreeing in some one thing—sometimes, indeed, in the fact that they are referred to one principle. Thus a thing is called *military* either because it is a military man's instrument—a sword, perhaps—or because it is his clothing, such as a cuirass, or because it is his vehicle, for example, a horse. But sometimes those concepts agree in being all referred to one end, as medicine is called *healthy* because it produces health, diet because it conserves health, urine because it indicates health. In other instances, however, terms agree according to different proportions to the same subject, as a quality is called a *being* because it is a disposition of per se being, namely, of substance, quantity because it is a measure of substance, and so forth.[17] Finally, the terms may agree according to one proportion to diverse subjects.[18] Thus sight is in relation to the body what intellect is in relation to the soul, so that just as sight is a power of a bodily organ, so intellect is a power of the soul in which the body does not participate. Aristotle therefore says that *good* is predicated of many things, not through concepts completely different, as with things equivocal

---

16. Commentary on Aristotle's *Nicomachean Ethics* (I *Eth.*, 7, 95 f. Numbering is that of the Pirotta edition).

17. The three kinds of predication signalized above are all cases of analogy of proportion or attribution. Note that the first two examples are of predicates intrinsically and formally univocal; the third of a predicate intrinsically and formally analogical.

18. I.e., they may agree according to analogy of proper proportionality.

purely by chance, but rather by way of analogy, that is, by the same proportion, seeing that all goods depend upon one first principle of goodness, or are all ordered to one end. For Aristotle did not mean that that separated Good was the idea and intelligible form *(ratio)* of all goods, but their principle and end. Or, again, all things are said to be good according to analogy or the same proportion in this way, that just as sight, for example, is a good of the body, so intellect is a good of the soul. Indeed Aristotle prefers this third mode of analogy[19] because it is based upon the goodness inhering in things. In the first two modes, involving as they do predication in respect to the *separated* good, a thing is not so properly denominated *good* as it is in the third one.[20]

2. Applications: The Problem of the Analogical Community Between Creatures and God

It[21] must be said that nothing can be predicated univocally of the creature and God; for in all univocals the intelligible nature signified by the name *(ratio nominis)* is common to each of the things of which that name is univocally predicated. Thus, with respect to that nature, univocals are equal, although in its actual existence one can be prior or posterior to another. For example, so far as the concept of number itself is concerned, all numbers are on a par, yet in fact one number may be prior to another. Now, however much it may imitate God, no creature can ever attain to this, that anything the same in its very intelligible essence should be common to it and to God. For,

---

19. Proper proportionality.

20. This conclusion follows from the fact that analogy of proper proportionality consists in the intrinsic proportional participation of a common perfection, whereas analogy of proportion or attribution, considered as such, apart from the not infrequent co-presence of the former analogy, does not.

21. The following section is taken from *De Ver.,* II, 11.

those things which, as regards the same intelligible essence, are present in diverse subjects, are common to them in point of substance [second substance] or of quiddity, but are distinct in point of existence *(esse)*. But whatever is in God *is* His own proper act of existing; for just as essence in Him is the same as act of existing, so science *(scientia),* for example, is the same in Him as His actual scientific knowing *(scientem esse)*. Consequently, since the act of existing proper to one thing cannot be communicated to another, it is impossible that the creature should have anything in common with God quidditatively, even as it cannot possibly acquire the same act of existing as His. Similarly in our case: if for instance in Peter, man and the act of being a man did not differ, it would be impossible to predicate *man* univocally of Peter and Paul, whose very existences are diverse.[22] Yet it cannot be asserted that whatever is predicated of God and creature is predicated in a purely equivocal sense, because if there existed no real likeness of creature to God, God's essence would not be the likeness of created things, and thus in knowing His own essence, He would not know creatures. Likewise, in that case we would be unable to attain to any knowledge of God from creatures. Nor, then, among names befitting creatures[23] would any one of them be predicable of Him in preference to any other; for in regard to terms purely equivocal it matters not what name be used, seeing that there is no likeness in reality between them. Therefore it must be said that the name *science*[24] is said of God's science and of ours neither in an altogether univocal sense, nor purely equivocally, but by way of analogy; which simply means according to a proportion.

Now proportional likeness can be twofold, giving rise to a double community of analogy. 1) There exists a certain conformity

---

22. Thus it is clear that univocal predication itself rests upon diversity in act of existing, and consequently upon the analogy of being in exercised act.

23. And all our words are derived from our knowledge of creatures.

24. Or any other name properly predicated of God and creature.

among things proportioned to each other because of a mutual determinate distance or some other [determinate] relation between them, as two is proportioned to one by being the double of one. 2) Sometimes we find a mutual conformity of two things between which there is no [determinate] proportion, but rather a mutual likeness of two proportions; e.g., six is "like" four in this, that just as six is the double of three, so four is the double of two. The first kind of conformity is thus one of proportion, the second, of proportionality. So, in accordance with that first kind of conformity we find something predicated analogically of two things one of which is related to the other, as being *(ens)* is said of substance and of accident through the relation that substance and accident have to each other, and as *healthy* is predicated of urine and of animal because urine has a certain likeness[25] to the health of the animal. But sometimes a term is predicated analogically according to the second kind of conformity [proportionality], as the name *vision* is said of corporeal vision and of intellectual vision by reason of the fact that just as sight is in the eye, so intellect is in the soul. [As was said], in things predicated analogically in the first way [according to proportion] there must be some determinate relation between the entities to which a term is common by analogy. It is therefore impossible for anything to be said of God and creature by this mode of analogy. For no creature has a relation to God such that, through it, the divine perfection could be determined.[26] But in the second mode of analogy no determinate relation exists between those things to which something is common by analogy. Therefore nothing prevents some name from being predicated analogically of God and creature according to this mode of analogy.

25. That of a sign or an indication.
26. Note that St. Thomas does not argue here that "analogy of proportion" can in no sense obtain between the creature and God, but he does exclude this analogy in what he apparently takes to be the strict and proper sense of it, as involving some mutual *determinate* relation.

There are, however, two modes of predication by way of proportionality. 1) Sometimes the name to be predicated implies in its primary meaning something respecting which no likeness can obtain between God and creature. . . . Such is the case in all things predicated of God symbolically, as when words like *lion* or *sun* are said of Him.[27] For in the definition of such terms is included matter—which cannot be attributed to God. 2) Sometimes the name predicated of God and creature involves in its principal signification nothing that could prevent the aforesaid mode of community [proportionality] from existing between the creature and God. Such is the case with all names whose definition entails no imperfection,[28] nor any actual dependence upon matter. This [absence of limitation] we find in the terms being, good, and the like.[29]

3. THE BASIS OF METAPHYSICAL ANALOGY: DIVERSITY IN ACT OF EXISTING

. . . two principles are to be considered in a thing, namely, its nature or quiddity and its act of existing. Now in all univocals there must be community according to nature and not according to act of existing, because one act of existing only is present in each thing. Thus human nature does not exist in two men according to the same act of existing. So it is that when the form signified by a name is the act of existing itself *(ipsum esse)*, it cannot appertain

---

27. Symbolic or metaphorical predication is therefore called "analogy of improper proportionality." The predicates are univocal in their proper meanings and are simply transferred to diverse subjects because of a certain proportional likeness of a dynamical character between them. Cf. James F. Anderson, *The Bond of Being,* Part Three.

28. And thus no limitation.

29. I.e., in transcendental terms, which are intrinsically analogical by analogy of proper proportionality.

to things univocally; neither therefore is being *(ens)* predicated univocally.[30]

The act of existing of each and every being is proper to it and is distinct from the act of existing of every other being.[31]

Diversity with respect to act of existing prevents the univocal predication of being *(ens)*. . . . A diverse way of existing *(diversus modus existendi)* bars such predication.[32]

---

30. *I Sent.*, XXXV, 1, 4. Observe the analogical use of "form" in this sentence. The act of existing can be called a "form" only in virtue of a certain proportional likeness, the act of existing having proportionally, and only proportionally, the same status and role vis-à-vis essence as does form vis-à-vis matter.

31. *De Pot.*, VII, 3.

32. *De Pot.*, VII, 7.

V

GENERAL INTRODUCTION TO THE TRANSCENDENTALS

1. Their Place Among The Divine Names

THE NAMES *being* and *good, one* and *true,* are prior to the other divine names in the order of understanding absolutely considered. This is clear from their universality *(communitas).* They can however be compared with each other in two ways: 1) with respect to subject *(suppositum),* and so viewed, they are mutually convertible, being identical in their subject [*ens*] . . . , or 2) with respect to their concepts, and considered thus, being *(ens)* is simply and absolutely prior to the others. It is so because being is included in the concept of the others, but not conversely. For the first object envisaged by the intellect is being, without which nothing can be apprehended by it, just as the first object of intellectual conviction is first principles, and especially this one: that contradictories are not simultaneously true. Thus all the other [divine names] are somehow included in being, unitedly and indistinctly, as in their source. And for this reason, too, it is fitting that *being* should be the most proper of the divine names. However, the other names we mentioned—*good, true* and *one*—do add "something" to being, not indeed any essence or nature at all, but only a certain intelligible aspect. Thus, *one* introduces the aspect of indivision; and it is because it adds to being only a negation that it is the closest [transcendental] to being. *True* and *good,* on the other hand, add to being a certain relation: good, a relation to an end; true, a relation to an exemplar form. For any thing whatever is said to be true in virtue of the fact that it imitates the divine exemplar or is in a relationship [of conformity] to a cognitive power; e.g., we speak of gold as being "true" because it has the form of gold which it manifests, and accordingly a true judgment is made about it. But if the transcendental properties of being [especially the good and the true] are considered under the aspect of causality, then the good is prior, because goodness has the nature of a final cause . . . , and the final cause in the order of causality.[1]

Now beauty and goodness are the same in subject . . . and differ only in reason . . . Whereas goodness has the character of a final cause, beauty properly pertains to the order of formal causality.[2]

2. DERIVATION OF THE TRANSCENDENTALS[3] FROM BEING

Just as in demonstrable matters a reduction must be made to principles intrinsically evident to the intellect, so likewise in investigating what any thing is; else one will fall into a regress infinite in both directions, with the result that the science and knowledge of things will perish utterly. Now that which the intellect first conceives, as inherently its most intelligible object, and to which it reduces all conceptions, is being (ens), as Avicenna says in the beginning of his Metaphysics.[4] Consequently all other conceptions of the intellect must be arrived at by addition to being. Nothing, however, can be added to being as an extraneous nature, in the manner in which a difference is added to a genus or an accident to a subject, because every nature is essentially being.[5] It is for this reason also that the

1. *I Sent.*, VIII, 1, 3.
2. *ST* I, 5, 4, ad 1, with I-II, 27, 1, ad 3.
3. Except beauty. This entire section is from *De Ver.*, I, 1.
4. Tract 1, bk. 2, ch. 1 (Venetiis, 1495, p. 5, col. 2).
5. Nothing is 'outside' being, except non-being, while the specific difference and the accident are as such extrinsic to the genus and the subject respectively.

Philosopher in the third book of the *Metaphysics*[6] proves that being cannot be a genus. But some things are said to be added over and above being in so far as they express a mode of being which the term being does not itself express. This is possible in two ways.

In one way, so that the mode expressed be some special mode of being. For there are diverse grades of entity corresponding to diverse modes of existing *(modi essendi)*, and in accordance with these modes the diverse genera of things are obtained. Thus, substance does not add over and above being any differentiating character, which would signify some sort of nature superadded to being. Rather, a certain special mode of being is expressed by the word *substance*, namely, being-through-itself *(per se ens);* and so it is as regards the other genera.

In a second way, so that the mode expressed is a mode consequent to every being in general. And this general mode, in turn, can be taken in two ways: 1) as that which follows upon every being, in itself; 2) as that which follows upon every being in relation to something else. If taken in the first of these ways, it is because the mode expresses something in the being affirmatively or negatively. But there is nothing affirmatively expressed and predicable absolutely of every being except its essence, according to which it is said to be.[7] And thus the word *thing (res)* is imposed, which according to Avicenna in the beginning of his *Metaphysics*[8] differs from being in this, that being is taken from the act of existing *(actus essendi)*, whereas the name *thing (res)* expresses the quidity or essence of being *(ens)*.

On the other hand, the negation consequent upon every being, as such, is indivision;[9] and the word *one (unum)* expresses this. For

6. 998b 22.
7. A thing is said to be "according to its essence" inasmuch as it is through and in its essence that the thing exists. But St. Thomas' phrase here cannot be taken to suggest that the essence confers the *esse*.
8. Tract 1, bk. 2, ch. 1 *(op. cit.,* p. 6, col. 1).
9. Undividedness or integrity.

one is nothing other than undivided being *(ens indivisum)*. But if taken in the second of the aforesaid ways, that is, according to the order of one thing to another, the general mode of being again can be considered in twofold fashion. 1) According to the division of one thing from another; and this is expressed by the word *something (aliquid)*, as if to say *some other thing (quasi aliud quid)*. Accordingly, just as being is called *one* inasmuch as it is undivided in itself, so it is called *something* inasmuch as it is divided from[10] others. 2) With respect to the conformity of one being to any thing else; and such conformity cannot exist unless there be something whose nature it is to accord with every being. This, however, is the soul which, as is said in the third book of *The Soul,*[11] is in a certain way all things. But in the soul there is a cognitive power and an appetitive power. The word *good (bonum)*, then, expresses the conformity of being to appetite; as stated in the beginning of the *Ethics*, "The good is what all desire."[12] The word *true (verum)*, however, expresses the conformity of being to intellect.

---

10. I.e., exists as a distinct entity apart from. . . .
11. Aristotle, *De An.*, III, 431b 21.
12. *Eth. Nicom.*, I, 1 (1094a 2 f.)

VI

THE TRANSCENDENTAL: *ONE*

1. Does *one* Add Anything to *being?*[1]

OBJECTIONS. 1. It seems that *one (unum)* adds something to *being (ens)*. For everything in a determinate genus exists so by addition to being, which encompasses all genera. But *one* is in a determinate genus, for it is the principle of number, which is a species of quantity. Therefore *one* adds something to *being*.

2. Further, that which divides something common is related to it by addition. But being is divided by *one* and by *many*. Therefore *one* adds something to *being*.

3. Again, if *one* does not add to *being*, *one* and *being* must have identically the same meaning. But to call *being* by the name of *being* would be vain, useless. Therefore it would be equally so to call being *one*. Now this is false. Consequently *one* does add something to *being*.

On the contrary, Dionysius says: "Nothing exists that is not in some way one."[2] This would not be true if *one* added to *being* in the sense of limiting it. Therefore *one* is not an addition to *being*.

I answer: *One* does not add any reality to being, but is only the negation of division; for *one* simply means undivided being. It is clear from this very fact that *one* is convertible with *being*. For every

---

1. *ST* I, 11, 1.
2. *De Div. Nom.*, V, 2 (PG 3, 977).

being is either simple or composite. But what is simple is undivided both actually and potentially; whereas the composite has no being as such so long as its parts remain separately existent but only after they come together to make up and compose it. Manifestly, therefore, the actual being *(esse)* of every thing that is consists in indivision.[3] And so it is that everything guards its unity as it guards its very existence *(esse)*.

Answers to Objections. 1. Some, thinking that the *one* convertible with *being* is the same as the *one* which is the principle of number, maintained contrary opinions. Pythagoras and Plato, seeing that the *one* convertible with *being* did not add any reality to being, but signified the substance of being as undivided, thought that the same applied to the *one* which is the principle of number.[4] And because number is composed of unities, they believed that numbers were the substances of all things. On the contrary, however, Avicenna, considering that the *one* which is the principle of number added a reality to the substance of being (otherwise number made of unities would not be a species of quantity), believed that the *one* convertible with being adds a certain reality over and above the substance of a being; as white adds to man.[5] But this is manifestly false, because each and every thing is one through its substance. For if a thing were one by anything other than its substance, since this again would be one supposing it were again one by something else, we should be driven on to infinity. Hence the former statement must be adhered to. It must be said, then, that the *one* which is convertible with being does not add a reality to being, but that the *one* which is the principle of number does add to being something pertaining to the genus of quantity.

2. Nothing prevents a thing which in one way is divided from being in another way undivided. Thus what is divided

---

3. I.e., in its existential oneness or integrity.
4. Cf. Aristotle, *Metaph.,* I (A), 5 (987a 13); 6 (987b 23).
5. *Metaph.,* III, 3 (791).

in number may be undivided in species. So it may be that a thing is in one way *one,* and in another way *many.* Nevertheless, if a thing is absolutely undivided, either because it is so according to what belongs to its essence (though it may be divided as regards things extrinsic to its essence, as what is one in subject may have many accidents), or because it is undivided actually and divided potentially (as what is one in the whole and many in its parts), then in such cases the thing will be one absolutely and many in a certain respect.[6]

On the other hand, a thing may be undivided in a certain respect and divided absolutely. Thus, while divided in essence, a thing could be undivided in idea or in principle or cause; in which case it will be many absolutely and one in a certain respect, as are things many in number and one in species or in principle. It is in this way that being is divided by *one* and *many*: by *one* absolutely and by *many* in a certain respect. For multitude itself would not be contained under being unless it were in some way contained under unity. As Dionysius says: "There is no kind of multitude that is not in a way one. But what are many in their parts are one in their whole; and what are many in accidents are one in subject; and what are many in number are one in species; and what are many in species are one in genus; and what are many in processions are one in principle."[7]

3. It does not follow that it is nugatory to say *being* is *one;* for *one* adds something to *being* logically.

The[8] one and the many which divide being are not the same as the one that is the principle of number nor as the many which is a species of quantity. . . . For it does not pertain to a thing that is contained under an inferior to be a difference *(differentia)* of the superior; thus rational is not a difference of substance. Consequently, the

---

6. One *simpliciter* and many *secundum quid.*

7. *De Div. Nom.,* XIII, 2 (PG 3, 980).

8. The following paragraphs concluding this section are taken from *I Sent.,* XXIV, 1, 3.

kind of multitude which falls under quantity cannot be a difference of being taken absolutely.[9] Hence they[10] say that the one convertible with being adds nothing positively to a thing, because a thing is not said to be one through any added disposition. For if that disposition also, being one, were again one by some other unity, we would lapse into an infinite regress. They state, therefore, that unity includes in its concept being in general, and adds over and above being the notion of a certain privation or negation, namely, indivision. Thus, like all terms signifying identically the same reality and differing only in reason, *being* and *one* are convertible, *one* adding to *being* only a negation. Considered precisely in respect of what it adds to being, the concept of unity then expresses a negation pure and simple, and so likewise *multitude* adds to *many-things* only a certain intelligible note, namely, that of division. For just as a thing is said to be *one* because it is not divided, so things are said to be *many* because they are divided.

But the primary ground of the division whereby one thing is distinguished from another lies in affirmation and negation. So it is that multitude includes in its very meaning negation, inasmuch as manyness results from the fact that one thing is *not* another. And the negation of this mode of division, which constitutes the essence of multitude, is precisely what is entailed in the concept of unity. Thus understood, unity and multiplicity are among the primary differentiae of being, according to which being is divided into *one* and *many,* and into act and potency. Hence, taken in this sense, one and many are not limited to any genus. The multitude here in question, then, is not that kind of number which is a species of quantity, nor is this unity the unity which is the principle of number. . . . I say then that number and unity, in the genus of quantity, are found

9. Rational is inferior in relation to animal, but animal itself comes under substance. Thus "rational" is not a specific difference of substance. Similarly, quantitative multitude is subsumed under quantity, but quantity is itself "inferior to" being as such, since it is a mode of it.

10. St. Thomas is referring to Aristotle and Averroes.

only in things quantitatively measurable, and therefore only in things having continuous quantity. Hence the Philosopher says that we know number by the division of the continuous; and number in this sense only, is the subject of arithmetic. . . .[11] Consequently number and unity of this sort are not predicated of divine things, but only unity and multitude consequent upon being universally.[12] So it is that in divine things terms like these add nothing logically to the reality they are predicated of, except the note of mere negation, as the Master of the *Sentences* states.[13]

2. Are One and Many Opposed to Each Other?[14]

Objections. 1. It seems that *one* and *many* are not mutually opposed. For no opposite is predicated of its opposite. But every multitude is in some way one, as is clear from the preceding Article. Therefore *one* is not opposed to *multitude*.

2. Further, no opposite is constituted by its opposite. But multitude is constituted by unity, which therefore is not opposed to multitude.

3. Further, each thing has one opposite. But the opposite of *many* is *few*. Therefore the opposite of *many* is not *one*.

4. Further, if *one* is opposed to multitude, it is opposed as the undivided is to the divided, and is thus opposed to it as a privation to a habitus. But this appears to be incongruous; because then it would follow that *one* is posterior to multitude and is defined by it; whereas, on the contrary, *multitude* is defined by *one*. Hence there would be a vicious circle in the definition [of these terms]; which is inadmissible. Therefore *one* and *many* are not opposed.

11. *Cf. Metaph.,* XIII (M), 8 (1083b 16).
12. I.e., the transcendentals *one* and *many* which divide being.
13. *Sent.,* I, 24.
14. *ST* I, 11, 2.

On the contrary, things opposed in their intelligible essences (*rationes*) are themselves opposed to each other. But the essence of unity consists in indivisibility, while that of multitude involves division. Therefore *one* and *many* are opposed to each other.

I answer: *One* is opposed to *many*, but in diverse ways. The *one* which is the principle of number is opposed to the multitude which is number, as the measure is to the thing measured. For *one* has the nature of a primary measure, and number is multitude measured by *one,* as is clear from the tenth book of the *Metaphysics.*[15] But the *one* which is convertible with being is opposed to multitude by way of privation; as the undivided is to the divided.

Answers to objections. 1. No privation takes away the being of a thing totally; for, as the Philosopher says,[16] a privation is a "negation in a subject." Nevertheless every privation takes away some actual being *(esse)*. And thus, by reason of being's actual universality *(communitas),* a privation of being has its foundation in being; which is not the case in privations of special forms, such as the privation of sight, or of whiteness, and the like. And what is true of being is true also of unity and goodness, which are convertible with being, for the privation of good is founded in some good, just as the removal of unity is founded in something one. And so it turns out that multitude is a certain unity, and evil a certain good, and non-being a certain being.[17] Nevertheless, an opposite is not predicated of an opposite, since one of them is absolute and the other relative. For what is being in a relative mode (i.e., in potency) is non-being absolutely (i.e., actually); or what is being in the absolute sense, in the genus of substance, is non-being relatively, as regards some accidental act of being *(esse accidentale).* Similarly, then, what is relatively good [good in some respect] is absolutely bad [bad in itself], or vice versa. Likewise, what is absolutely one is relatively many, and vice versa.

15. Cf. *Metaph.,* X (I), 1 (1052b 18).
16. *Op. cit.,* IV (Γ), 2 (1004a 15).
17. I.e., in relation to their subjects.

2. A whole is twofold. One kind of whole is homogeneous, composed of like parts; another is heterogeneous, composed of dissimilar parts. Now in every homogeneous whole, the whole is made up of parts having the form of the whole; every part of water, for instance, is water; and such is the constitution of a continuous thing made up of its parts. On the other hand, in every heterogeneous whole, each part lacks the form belonging to the whole; thus no part of a house is a house, nor is any part of man a man. Now a multitude is such a kind of whole. Therefore, inasmuch as the multitude's part does not possess the form of the multitude, the latter is composed of unities, as a house is composed of non-houses; not indeed as if unities constituted multitude so far as the unities are undivided (in which respect they are opposed to multitude), but so far as they have entity; as also the parts of a house make up the house by the fact that they are bodies, not by the fact that they are not houses.

3. *Many* is taken in two ways; 1) absolutely, and in this sense it is opposed to *one;* 2) as importing a certain excess, in which sense it is opposed to *few.* Hence in the first sense two are many, but not in the second sense.

4. *One* is opposed to *many* privatively, inasmuch as the latter implies division. Hence division must be prior to unity, not absolutely in itself, but according to our way of apprehension. For we apprehend simple things through composite things. Thus we define a point as that which has no part, or as the beginning of a line. Multitude also, in idea, follows on unity; because we do not understand divided things to have the nature of a multitude except by the fact that we attribute unity to every single one of them. Hence *one* is placed in the definition of *multitude,* but *multitude* is not placed in the definition of *one.* Division, however, comes to be understood from the very negation of being. So, what first comes to the intellect is being; secondly, that this being is *not* that being, and thus we apprehend division as a consequence; thirdly, comes the notion of *one;* fourthly, the notion of multitude.

3. Is God One?[18]

Objections. 1. It seems that God is not one. For it is written: "For there be many gods and many lords" (*I Cor.* 8:5).

2. Further, *one,* as the principle of number, cannot be predicated of God, because quantity is not predicated of God; neither can the one which is convertible with being be predicated of God, because it imports privation, and every privation is an imperfection, and there is no imperfection in God. Therefore God is not one.

On the contrary, it is written: "Hear, O Israel, the Lord our God is one Lord" (*Deut.,* 6:4).

I answer: It can be shown from three sources that God is one. First, from His simplicity. For it is manifest that the reason why any singular thing is this particular thing is because it cannot be communicated to many. Thus, although that whereby Socrates is a man can be communicated to many, what makes him this particular man is communicable to one being only. Therefore, if Socrates were a man in virtue of what makes him to be this particular man, as there cannot be many Socrateses, so there could not in that way be many men. Now this belongs to God alone; for God Himself is His own nature, as was shown above.[19] Therefore in identically the same way God is God and this God. So it is impossible that there should be many gods.

Secondly, this is proved from the infinity of God's perfection. For it was shown above[20] that God comprehends in Himself the whole perfection of being *(totam perfectionem essendi).* Hence, if many gods existed, they would necessarily differ from each other, so that something would belong to one which did not belong to another. In this case, a perfection would be lacking in one of them, and the thing deprived of this perfection then would not be absolutely perfect. It is therefore impossible for many gods to exist. And

18. *ST* I, 11, 3.
19. Q. 3, a. 3.
20. Q. 4, a. 2.

thus when the ancient philosophers, compelled as it were by the truth, asserted an infinite principle, they asserted likewise that there was only one such principle.

Thirdly, this is shown from the unity of the world. For all things that exist are seen to be ordered to each other since some serve others. But things mutually diverse do not come together in the same order unless they be ordered thereto by some single being. For many are reduced into one order by one thing better than by many: because what is one is the essential cause of what is one, while the many are the cause of the one only accidentally, i.e., so far as they themselves are in some way one. Since, then, what is first is most perfect, and is so essentially and not accidentally, it must be that the first which reduces all into one order is only one. And this is God.

Answers to Objections. 1. Gods are called many by the error of certain persons who worshipped many deities, believing as they did that the planets and other stars were gods, and even particular parts of the world. Wherefore the Apostle adds: "Our God is one," etc. (*I Cor.* 8:6).

2. The *one* which is the principle of number is not predicated of God, but only of things existing in matter. For the *one* which is the principle of number belongs to the genus of mathematical objects, which have existence in matter but are abstracted from matter in idea. But the one that is convertible with being is a metaphysical reality which does not existentially depend on matter. And although in God there is no privation, nevertheless, according to the mode of our apprehension, He is known by us only by way of privation and remotion. Thus there is no reason why certain privative terms should not be predicated of God; for instance, that He is incorporeal, and infinite; and in this same way [privatively] it is said of God that He is *one*.

VII

THE TRANSCENDENTAL: *TRUE*

I. What is Truth?[1]

O BJECTIONS. 1. Now it seems that truth is absolutely the same as being, for Augustine says in his *Soliloquies*,[2] that the true is that which is. But that which is, is nothing other than being *(ens)*. Therefore *true* signifies absolutely the same as *being*.

2. In answer to this it was said that truth and being are the same in reality,[3] but differ in "idea"—differ in their intelligible nature.[4] But on the contrary, the intelligible nature of anything is that which is signified by its definition. However, after having rejected certain other definitions, that-which-is is given by Augustine as the definition of truth. Therefore, since truth and being are one with respect to that-which-is, it seems that they are the same in idea.[5]

3. Further, things that differ in idea are related to each other in such a way that one of them can be apprehended without the other. Wherefore Boethius says in the *De Hebdomadibus*,[6] that it is possible to grasp God's being *(Deus esse)* if His goodness be separated by the

1. *De Ver.,* I, 1; cf. *ST* I, 16, 3.
2. II, 5 (PL 32, 889).
3. *Secundum supposita,* i.e., in their subjects. Note that suppositality has a meaning radically opposed to the usual modern one of "subjectivity" as implying psychological relativism.
4. *Secundum rationem.*
5. *Idem ratione,* i.e., the same in their intelligible essence or nature.
6. PL 64, 1312.

intellect for a moment. But being can in no wise be known by the intellect in separation from truth, because being is grasped by the fact that it is true. Therefore truth and being do not differ in idea.

4. Further, if truth is not the same as being, it must be a disposition of being. But it cannot be a disposition of being. For 1) it is not a totally corrupting disposition; otherwise it would follow: This is true, therefore it is a non-entity, just as it follows: The man is dead, therefore the man is not. Similarly 2) truth is not a diminishing disposition; otherwise it would not follow: This is true, therefore it is; just as it does not follow: This person is white with respect to teeth, therefore he is white. Again, 3) truth does not contract or specify being, since it would not then be convertible with being. Therefore truth and being are altogether the same.

5. Further, things whose disposition is the same are the same. But the disposition of truth and of being is the same. Hence they are the same. For it is said in the second book of the *Metaphysics:* "The disposition of a thing in being is the same as its disposition in truth."[7] Therefore truth and being are wholly the same.

6. Things not the same differ in some respect. But truth and being in no way differ. For they do not differ in essence, since being is true by its essence. Nor do they even differ by other differences, for it would be necessary that they should agree in some genus. Therefore they are entirely the same.

7. Further, if truth and being are not altogether the same, then truth must add something to being. But the true adds nothing to being, even though the term *true* is greater in extension than *being*. This is clear from the Philosopher's statement in the fourth book of the *Metaphysics:* "Defining the true we say that what is, is, or that what is not, is not."[8] Thus truth includes being and non-being. Hence *true* does not add to *being*, and so it seems to be entirely the same as being.

---

7. Cf. Aristotle, *Metaph.,* II (α), 1 (993b 30).
8. *Metaph.,* IV (Γ), 7 (1011b 25 ff.).

1. On the contrary, however, useless repetition is vain. If, therefore, truth were the same as being, it would be nugatory to say "true being"; which is false. Therefore truth and being are not the same.

2. Further, being and good are convertible. But the true is not convertible with the good, for something may be true which is not good, as that this man commits fornication. Therefore truth is not convertible with being.

3. Further, Boethius says in the *De Hebdomadibus* that in all creatures being *(esse)* and what-is *(quod est)* are diverse.[9] But truth follows upon the act of existing *(esse)* of things. Therefore in creatures truth is diverse from what-is. But what-is *(quod est)* is the same as being *(ens)*. Therefore truth in creatures is diverse from being.

4. Further, things related to each other as prior and posterior must be diverse. But truth and being are so related, for, as is said in the *Book of Causes*,[10] "The first of created things is existence *(esse),*" and the Commentator, on that same book, says: "All other things are predicated as informing being *(per informationem de ente)*."[11] And thus they are posterior to being. Therefore truth and being are diverse.

5. Further, things predicated in common of a cause and of things caused are in a higher degree one in the cause than in the things caused, and especially is this true of God in comparison with creatures. But in God these four: *being, one, true, good,* are appropriated in such a manner that *being (ens)* pertains to the essence, *one* to the person of the Father, *true* to the person of the Son, *good* to the person of the Holy Ghost. But the divine persons are distinguished not only in reason but also in reality; hence they are not predicated of each other. Consequently, in creatures these four principles are all

---

9. PL 64, 1311.

10. Direct quotation from the Latin version of the *De Causis* used by St. Thomas in his *Expositio in Librum de Causis; Opera Omnia,* Parma edition, XX, 724 (*lectio* 4).

11. This Commentary of Averroes' is extremely rare and I have been unable to consult it.

the more surely bound to differ to a greater extent than merely logically.

I answer:[12] All knowledge is brought about by the assimilation of the knower to the thing known, so that the assimilation is said to be the cause of the knowledge. Thus sight knows color through the fact that it is disposed to the species of color. Therefore, the primary relation of being to intellect consists in the one's corresponding to the other; which correspondence is called the adequation of the thing and the intellect. And in this the notion of truth is realized formally. It is this, then, that truth adds to being: conformity or adequation of thing and intellect; and upon this conformity, as was said, knowledge of the thing follows. Thus the entity of the thing precedes truth formally so called;[13] but knowledge is a certain effect of truth.

Accordingly, truth and the true, it is found, are defined in three ways. In one way, with respect to that which precedes the formal notion of truth and upon which truth is based. Thus we have Augustine's definition:[14] "The true is that which is"; and Avicenna's,[15] "The truth of anything is a property of its existence which is established in it"; and a certain other definition states: "Truth consists in the unity of being and essence." In another way truth is defined according to that which constitutes its essence formally; and thus Isaac[16] says that "Truth is the adequation of thing and intellect"; and Anselm states:[17] "Truth is rightness perceptible to the mind alone." For this rightness is so called from a certain

---

12. See Chap. V, 1, for the first part of this *Respondeo*.

13. The *ratio veritatis*, which consists in the aforesaid relation of correspondence or adequation.

14. *Soliloquies*, II, 5 (PL 32, 889).

15. *Metaph.*, VIII, 6 (100r).

16. Isaac Israeli (Isaac Ben Salomon). On this classic definition, attributed to Isaac, see J. T. Muckle, C.S.B., "Isaac Israeli's Definition of Truth" (*Archives d'hist. doct. et litt. du moyen âge*, viii, 1933, pp. 5–8).

adequation according to which the Philosopher in the fourth book of the *Metaphysics* says: "Defining the true we assert that that which is, is, or that that which is not, is not."[18] In a third way [the relation of] truth is defined according to the effect consequent upon it. Thus Hilary lays it down that "Truth is manifestive and declarative being";[19] and Augustine in *The True Religion*[20] states: "Truth is that by which that which is, is shown forth"; and in the same work[21] he writes: "Truth is that according to which we judge concerning inferior things."

Answers to objections. 1. This definition of Augustine's is of truth according to its foundation in the real, not according to that whereby the notion of truth is fulfilled in the adequation of thing to intellect. Or, it must be added that when it is said, "Truth is that which is," truth is not taken there as it signifies the act of existing but rather as it is the name of the composite understanding, that is, as signifying the affirmation of a proposition; so that the statement actually means this: there is truth when that which is, is said to be. Thus Augustine's definition comes to the same as that of the Philosopher recorded above.[22]

The answer to the second is obvious from what has just been said.

3. For something to be known "without another" can be taken in two ways. In one way so that something is grasped when the other thing is not; and thus those things which differ in idea are so related to each other that one can be known without the other. In another way, a thing can be apprehended "without something else" which is known when the other does not exist; and in this way being cannot be understood "without" the true, because being

---

17. *De Veritate*, XI (PL 158, 480).
18. *Metaph.*, IV G, 7 (1011b 25–29).
19. *De Trin.*, V (PL 10, 131).
20. *De Vera Relig.*, XXXVI (PL 34, 151).
21. *Op. cit.*, (PL 34, 147).
22. Viz., that truth consists in saying that what is, is, and that what is not, is not.

cannot be grasped without that which corresponds or is adequated to the intellect. Yet it is not necessary that whosoever knows the nature of being knows the nature of truth, just as not everyone cognizant of being, is cognizant of the agent intellect, although without the agent intellect man can know nothing.

4. Truth is a disposition of being, not as adding some nature to it, nor as expressing some special mode of being, but as something universally found in being, which however is not expressed by the word *being*. Therefore truth need not be a disposition corrupting or diminishing or in any way contracting being.

5. Disposition is not taken there according as it is in the genus of quality, but as importing a certain order. Now those things which are the cause of the existence of others are in the highest degree beings, and those things which are the cause of the truth of other things are in the highest degree true. Hence the Philosopher concludes that the order of any thing is the same in actual being *(esse)* and in truth, so that where maximal being is found there also is found that which is supremely true. Nor is this so because being and truth are the same in idea, but because a thing is by its nature apt to be equated to an intellect by the very fact that it has something of entity. And thus the notion of truth follows that of being.

6. Truth and being differ in idea by the fact that something is contained in the notion of truth that is not contained in the notion of being. Yet they do not so differ that there is something in the notion of being that is not in the notion of truth. Nor do they differ in essence, nor are they distinguished from each other by opposed differences.

7. Truth is no greater in extension than being. For being, taken in a certain way, is predicated of non-being, according as non-being is apprehended by the intellect. Thus the Philosopher says in the fourth book of the *Metaphysics*[23] that negation or privation of being is in one sense called being. And in the beginning of his *Metaphysics*[24] Avicenna says, too, that it is not possible to form an

enunciation except of being, because that concerning which the proposition is formed must be apprehended by an intellect. From this it is obvious that every truth is in some mode a being.

Answers to objections to the contrary. 1. It is not tautological to speak of *true* being, because something is expressed by the word *true* which is not expressed by the word *being*; but they do not on that account differ in reality.

2. Although fornication is evil, nevertheless, according as this act possesses something of entity, it is by nature apt to be conformed to an intellect; and truth follows upon this conformity. And thus it is evident that truth neither exceeds nor is exceeded by being.

3. In the proposition, being and what-is are diverse, the act of existing *(actus essendi)* is distinguished from that to which that act belongs. The notion of being, however, is derived from the act of existing, not from that to which the act of existing belongs, and therefore the argument does not follow.[25]

4. Truth is posterior to being in this respect, that the notion of truth differs from that of being in the manner stated above.

5. This reasoning is defective in three respects. First, although the three divine persons are distinguished in reality, nevertheless the appropriations of the Persons do not differ really but only in reason. Second, although the Persons are really distinguished from each other, nevertheless they are not really distinguished from the divine act of existing whereby they are, and therefore neither is the *true* which is appropriated to the person of the Son distinguished really from the divine act of existing maintained on the part of the divine essence. Third, although being, truth, unity, and goodness are

---

23. Cf. *Metaph.*, IV (Γ), 2 (1004a 15).

24. Tract 1, bk. 2, ch. 1.

25. St. Thomas is giving his own interpretation of the famous Boethian distinction between *esse* and *quod est*. It may be that in Boethius himself the distinction is rather between the concrete substance *("quod est")* and the abstract nature or form *("esse")* in which it participates. Cf. M. Roland-Gosselin, *Le "De Ente et Essentia,"* pp. 142 ff.

united more in God than in created things, nevertheless, from the fact that they are logically distinct in God it does not necessarily follow that they are also really distinct in creatures. For this situation arises in the case of things that are not by their own essence one in fact, such as wisdom and power—which, though one in God, are really distinct in creatures. But being, the true, the one, and the good have unity by their very own essence. Hence, wherever they are found, they are really one, although the unity of the Reality whereby they are united in God is more perfect than that whereby they are united in creatures.

2. Is Truth Found Principally in the Intellect Rather Than in Things?[26]

Objections. 1. It seems that it is not found principally in the intellect. For truth, as has been said, is convertible with being. But being is found principally[27] outside the soul. Therefore truth is also.

2. Moreover, things are in the soul not by their essence, but by their species,[28] as is said in the third book of *The Soul*.[29] If, therefore, truth is found principally in the soul, truth will not be the essence of the thing, but the likeness or species of it; and the true will be the species of the being existing outside the soul. But the species of a thing existing within the soul is not predicated of the thing outside the soul, just as it is not convertible with it. Hence, neither is the true convertible with being; which is false.

3. Further, everything existing in something follows that in which it exists. If, then, truth exists principally in the soul, the judgment of truth follows the estimation of the soul. And thus there will

---

26. *De Ver.*, I, 2.
27. I.e., in its principle or source.
28. I.e., by their intelligible, or sensible, form.
29. Cf. Aristotle, *De An.*, III, 8 (431b 29 ff.).

arise again the error of those ancient philosophers[30] who said that whatever seems true to anyone is true, and that two contradictories are true at the same time; which is absurd.

4. Again, if truth resides principally in the intellect, then something pertaining to the intellection of truth must be included in the definition of truth. But Augustine, in his *Soliloquies,*[31] condemns definitions such as the following: "That is true which is as it is seen to be"; for, according to this, what is not seen would not be true; which is obviously false in the case of the deeply hidden stones that are in the bowels of the earth. Similarly he rejects[32] the statement: "That is true which is as it appears to a knower who is willing and able to know"; because, according to this, a thing would not be true unless a knower willed to know it and could know it. The same objection, then, would hold against any other definitions wherein something appertaining to intellect was included. Therefore truth does not reside principally in the intellect.

On the contrary, the Philosopher says in the sixth book of the *Metaphysics:*[33] "There is no truth or falsity except in the mind."

Moreover, truth is the adequation of thing and intellect. But this adequation can exist only in an intellect. Therefore truth exists only in an intellect.

I answer: In terms predicated of many things by priority and posteriority that which receives by priority the common predication need not always be the cause of the others. Rather, that in which the essence of that common predicate is primarily realized is that which receives by priority the common predication. Thus the word *healthy* is predicated by priority of the animal, wherein health is primarily found, although medicine is called *healthy* inasmuch as it is productive of health. Therefore, when the term *true* is predi-

---

30. Some of the Sophists. E.g., cf. Plato's Dialogue: *Protagoras.*
31. II, 4 (PL 32, 887).
32. *Ibid.,* (888).
33. *Metaph.,* VI (E), 4 (1027b 25–27).

cated of a number of things by priority and posteriority, it must be predicated as prior of that in which the concept of truth is fully realized.

Now the fulfillment of every motion or operation lies in its end. The motion of the cognitive power, however, is terminated in the soul. For the known must be in the knower according to the mode of the knower. The motion of the appetitive faculty, on the other hand, is terminated in the thing. And it is for this reason that the Philosopher, in the third book of *The Soul,*[34] places a kind of circle in the acts of the soul, according to which a thing outside the soul moves the intellect and the thing apprehended moves the appetite, and the appetite then leads to the attainment of the thing whence the motion started. And because, as was pointed out in the preceding article,[35] the term *good* expresses ordination to appetite, *true* ordination to intellect, so it is that the Philosopher, in the sixth book of the *Metaphysics,*[36] states that good and evil are in things, truth and falsity in the mind.

Now, a thing is not said to be true except as it is adequated to an intellect. Therefore truth is found posterior in things and prior in the intellect. But it must be borne in mind that a thing is related in one fashion to the practical intellect and in another to the speculative. For the practical intellect causes things, and therefore it is the measure of things made by it; whereas the speculative intellect, being receptive of things, is in a certain way moved by things themselves, and in consequence things measure it. From this it is evident that the natural things from which our intellect receives knowledge measure our intellect—as is said in the tenth book of the *Metaphysics*[37]—, but they themselves are measured by the divine intellect, in Whom are all created things, just as all artifacts are in the intellect of the artificer. Thus the divine intellect measures but is

34. Cf. *De An.*, III, 10 (433a 18–20).
35. *De Ver.*, I, 1.
36. *Metaph.*, VI (E), 4 (1027b 25–27).

not measured; natural things measure and are measured; but our intellect is measured, and it does not measure natural things but only artificial things.[38]

A natural thing, then, set up between two intellects, is said to be true by an adequation to both; for, according to the divine intellect, it is said to be true so far as it fulfills that to which it is ordered by the divine intellect, as is made evident by Anselm in his book *On Truth*,[39] by Augustine in *The True Religion*,[40] and by Avicenna in the definition previously quoted, namely, "The truth of each thing is a property of the being which has been given to it."[41] On the other hand, as regards adequation to the human intellect, a natural thing is said to be *true* so far as it is naturally constituted to produce a true estimation of itself, just as, on the contrary, things are said to be *false* which are by nature apt to seem what they are not or as they are not, as is said in the fifth book of the *Metaphysics*.[42] The notion of truth, however, is by priority realized in the thing by the first relation [that of the thing to the divine intellect] rather than by the second one [that of the thing to the human intellect], because the relation to the divine intellect is prior to the human, so that even if the human intellect did not exist, things would still be said to be true in their relation to the divine intellect. But if both intellects were understood to be removed, which is impossible, the principle of truth would in no wise remain.

Answers to Objections. 1. It is obvious from the foregoing that truth is predicated of the intellect as prior and of the thing adequated to it as posterior. And in both ways it is convertible with being, but in diverse manners. 1) As said of things, truth is convertible with being by predication. (For every being is adequated to the

---

37. Aristotle, *Metaph.*, X (I), 1 (1058a 32).
38. Things made by human art.
39. Cf. *De Veritate*, VII (PL 158, 475).
40. Cf. *De Vera Religione*, XXXI, (PL 34, 150).
41. *Metaph.*, VIII, 6 (1001)—or *Metaph.*, VIII, 8, 6 (tract 8, bk. 8, ch. 6).
42. Aristotle, *Metaph.*, V (Δ), 29 (1024b 21 ff.).

divine intellect and can adequate the human intellect to itself, and conversely.) 2) But if truth is taken as predicated of intellect, it is convertible with extramental being, not by predication but by conformity, seeing that some being must accord with every intellect, and conversely.

And from this the solution to the second is clear.

3. What is in something does not follow that in which it is, except when it is caused by the principles of that thing. Thus light, which is caused in the air by something extrinsic, the sun, follows the motion of the sun rather than the air. Similarly, the truth that is caused in the soul by things does not follow upon the soul's judgment, but upon the existence of the things. For from the fact that the thing is or is not, utterance is said to be true or false, and the intellect for the same reason is said to be true or false.

4. Augustine is speaking of the vision of the human intellect, upon which the truth of the thing does not depend. For many things exist that are unknown to our intellect. But there is no thing that the divine intellect does not know actually and the human intellect does not know potentially; for the agent intellect is described as that whose function it is to make all things, and the possible intellect as that whose function it is to be made [or to become] all things. And therefore, in the definition of *true-thing* the divine intellect's vision-in-act can be placed, but not the human intellect's vision, except in potency, as appears from what has been said in the body of the article.

As[43] is clear from what has been stated above, truth is found properly in the intellect, human or divine, just as health is found properly in the animal. Now truth is found in other things through their relation to intellect, even as health is predicated of certain other things inasmuch as they are productive or conservative of the health of the animal. Truth, then, is properly and primarily in the

---

43. *De Ver.*, I, 4, c.

divine intellect; it is indeed properly, but secondarily, in the human
intellect; but in things it is improperly and secondarily, because
truth is not in things except in relation to one or the other of the
two truths of intellect. Thus the truth of the divine intellect is only
one, from which many truths in the human intellect are derived—
"just as from one man's face many likenesses are reflected in a mir-
ror," as the *Gloss* says[44] concerning the Psalmist's saying (*Ps.,* 11:2):
"Truths are decayed from among the children of men." The truths
that are in things, however, are as many as there are entities of
things. But the truth which is predicated of things in relation to the
human intellect is in a certain way accidental to the things; for,
supposing that the human intellect did not and could not exist,
things would still abide in their essence. But the truth which is
predicated of things in relation to the divine intellect is communicated to them inseparably; for they cannot subsist except by the divine intellect's bringing them forth into existence. Thus truth is
prior in the thing by relation to the divine intellect than by relation
to the human; for it is related to the divine intellect as to its cause,
but to the human intellect as, in a certain fashion, to its effect,
inasmuch as the [human] intellect receives its knowledge from
things. Therefore a thing is said to be true in a more originative,
more "principle," sense by virtue of its relation to the truth of
the divine intellect than to the truth of the human intellect.
Consequently, if truth properly so called is taken in the sense in
which all things are true in their principle, then all things are true
by one truth, namely, by the truth of the divine intellect. And it is
thus that Anselm speaks of truth in his dialogue, *On Truth.*[45] On the
other hand, if truth properly so called is taken in the sense in which
things are said to be true secondarily, or derivatively, then there are
many truths of many true things in different minds. But if truth is
taken in the improper sense according to which all things are said

44. Peter Lombard, *In Psalm.,* super XI, 2 (PL 191, 155); cf. St. Augustine, *Ennar.
in Psalm.,* super XI, 2 (PL 36, 138).

to be true, then there are many truths of many true things, yet there is only one truth of one thing.

Now things are denominated true [extrinsically] from the truth which is in the divine intellect or in the human intellect, as food is denominated healthful from the health which is in the animal, and not as by an inherent form. But by the truth that is in the thing itself (which is nothing other than the entity adequated to the intellect, or adequating the intellect to itself) things are denominated *true* as by an inherent form, just as food is denominated "healthful" by that quality existing in it in virtue of which it is called healthful.

45. *De Ver.,* VII and XIII (PL 158, 475, 486).

VIII

THE TRANSCENDENTAL: *GOOD*

1. Does *good* Add Something to *being*?[1]

OBJECTIONS. 1. It seems so. For each and every thing is a being *(ens)* by its essence. But the creature is not good by its essence, but by participation. Therefore goodness adds to being a certain reality.

2. Further, since goodness includes being in its concept, and is distinguished from being in idea, the concept of the good must add something to the concept of being. But it cannot be said that it adds a negation to being, as does unity, which adds indivision to being, because the whole notion of goodness consists in affirmation. Hence it adds affirmation *(positionem)* to being.

3. Yet it must be said that goodness adds a relation to the end. But on the contrary, in that case goodness would be nothing other than relative being. But such being belongs to a determinate genus of being, namely, relation. Thus the good is confined to a single determinate category; which is contrary to what the Philosopher says in the first book of the *Ethics,* where[2] he puts the good in all the categories.

4. Further, as can be gathered from what Dionysius says in the fourth chapter of *The Divine Names,*[3] the good diffuses its own

---

1. *De Ver.,* XXI, 1.
2. Cf. *Eth. Nicom.,* I, 6 (1096a 23 ff.).
3. Cf. *De Div. Nom.,* IV, 4; 20 (PG 3, 700; 720, with PG 3, 693, 697).

being. A thing then is good in virtue of the fact that it is self-diffusive. But diffusion entails a certain action. Action, however, proceeds from a thing's essence through the mediation of a power. Hence a thing is said to be good by reason of a power superadded to its essence. And thus goodness does add something over and above being.

5. Again, the farther from the single first simple Principle one recedes, the greater the distinctness found in things. But in God being and goodness are one really and distinct only in reason. So in creatures their distinction is greater than that of a distinction of reason; hence they are really distinct, since besides the distinction of reason, there is no other kind of distinction except the real.

6. Further, accidents add a reality to the essence. But goodness is accidental to the created thing; otherwise it could not lose its goodness. Therefore goodness adds something real over and above being.

7. Further, everything spoken of as in-forming something else adds a reality to that which it in-forms, since nothing is in-formed by itself. But the term *good* expresses a certain in-formation, as is said in the commentary on *The Book of Causes*.[4] Therefore goodness adds something to being.

8. Still it must be said that goodness determines being according to reason. But on the contrary, corresponding to that determination of reason there is either something real or nothing real. If the latter, it follows that the determination is vain and empty. On the other hand, if to that distinction of reason something real does correspond, then the proposition, *goodness adds something in reality to being,* is confirmed.

9. Further, a relation is specified according to that with reference to which it is predicated. But *good* is predicated with reference to a determinate genus, namely, the end. Therefore the term *good*

4. Cf. *De Causis,* XX (p. 177).

expresses a specific relation. Every specified entity, however, adds something really to being in general. Hence goodness adds a reality to being.

10. Again, just as goodness and being are convertible, so also are man and risibility. But although the latter is convertible with man, it nevertheless adds a reality to man, namely, a property, belonging therefore in the order of accidents. Hence goodness likewise adds a reality to being.

Objections to the Contrary. 1. There is Augustine's statement that, "inasmuch as God is good, we are; and inasmuch as we are, we are good."[5] Therefore it seems that goodness does not add something to being.

2. Further, if any things are so related that one adds something to another, either really or in reason, then one of them can be grasped without the other. But being cannot be cognized without the good. Therefore it adds nothing to being, either in reality or in reason. Proof of the minor: God can make more being than man can know. But God cannot make any being that is not good; for, from the fact that it is from the Good, it is good, as Boethius makes clear in the *De Hebdomadibus*.[6] Neither therefore can the intellect grasp *being* without grasping *good*.

I answer: Something can add to another in three ways. In one *way,* so that it adds a certain reality which is outside the essence of the thing to which it is said to be added. In this manner white adds to body, because the essence of whiteness is extrinsic to the essence of body. *In a second way,* something is said to add to another by limiting and determining it. In this way man adds something to animal, not indeed in the sense that there is in man any reality altogether outside the essence of animal; otherwise it would have to be said that man as a whole is not animal, but that animal is only a part of man. On the contrary, animal is limited by man in the sense that

5. *De Doct., Christ.,* I, 32 (PL 34, 32).
6. Cf. *De Hebdom.,* PL 64, 1313.

what is contained determinately and actually in the concept of man, is contained implicitly and as it were potentially in the concept of animal. Thus, it is of the essence of man that he have a rational soul, and of the essence of animal that it have a soul, though not necessarily a rational soul and not necessarily a non-rational one. However, this determination, by reason of which man is said to add to animal, is founded upon something real. *In a third way,* something is said to add to another only according to reason. This is the case when something is of the essence of one thing which is not of the essence of the other and this "something" has no being in the nature of things but only in reason, whether the thing it is said to be added to, be restricted by it, or not. Thus, *blind* adds something to *man,* namely, blindness, which is not a being existing in nature, but only a being of reason, in so far as "being" includes privations. And by this privation man is restricted, because not every man is blind. When, however, we speak of a mole as blind this addition effects no restriction.[7]

Now nothing can be added to universal being in the first way—by addition of something real—although some addition to some particular being can be made in that mode. The reason is that there is no thing of nature which is outside the essence of universal being, although some thing does exist outside the essence of this particular being. However, in the second way—by contraction and determination—there are certain things that add to being, because being is limited by the ten categories, each of which adds something over and above being—not indeed an accident, nor a differentia lying outside the essence of being, but rather a determinate mode of existing which is rooted in the very essence of the thing. But it is not in this way that goodness adds to being. For the good is divided into the ten categories just as being is—a point made clear in the first book of the *Ethics.*[8] Consequently, goodness either must add

7. The mole being blind by nature.
8. *Eth. Nicom.,* I, 6 (1096a 23 ff.).

nothing to being, or if it adds something, this must be according to reason only. For if goodness added something real it would follow necessarily that being was limited, by the notion of goodness, to some special genus. However, since being is that which first falls in the conception of the mind, as Avicenna says,[9] it follows of necessity that every name is either synonymous with being (which cannot be said of the term *good*, since it is not nugatory to predicate *good* of *being*), or adds something to being at least in idea. And so the good, by which being is not restricted, must add to being something pertaining to reason alone. But that which pertains to reason alone can be twofold only.[10] For every absolute affirmation signifies something existing in the nature of things.

So, then, to being (which is the first conception of the intellect) *one* adds that which pertains only to reason, namely, a negation; for *one* signifies *undivided* being. *True* and *good*, however, are said affirmatively; so that they can add to being only a relation of reason. Now, according to the Philosopher in the fifth book of the *Metaphysics*,[11] that relation is said to be one of reason alone, whereby what does not depend is said to be referred to its correlative; but when the relation itself is a certain dependency, it is real, as is evident in the case of the relation between knowledge and the knowable, or between sense and the sensible. For knowledge depends on the knowable and not conversely, so that the relation by which knowledge is referred to the knowable is real, while that by which the knowable is referred to knowledge is purely one of reason. Thus, according to the Philosopher, the knowable is said to be relative [or better, referable], not because it is itself referred to something else, but because something else is referred to it; and so it is with all other things that are related to each other as measure and measured, or as perfective and perfectible.

9. *Metaph.*, I, 6, fol. 72rb.
10. I.e., either a relation or a negation.
11. Cf. *Metaph.*, V (Δ), 15 (1021a 30 ff.).

Necessarily, then, the terms *true* and *good* add to the concept of being the aspect of perfectiveness. Now, in any being two things are to be considered: its specific intelligible nature or form *(ipsam rationem speciei),* and the very act of being by which it subsists in that nature. And so it is that a being can be perfective in two ways. *In one way,* as regards specification only,[12] and thus does being perfect the intellect according to the intelligible nature of being. Yet being is not present in the intellect according to its natural existence; and therefore this mode of perfecting adds the true to being. For truth is in the mind, as the Philosopher says in the sixth book of the *Metaphysics.*[13] And every being is said to be true to the extent that it is conformed or is conformable to an intellect; so that all who define truth rightly place intellect in the definition of it.

In a second way, a being is perfective of another not only as regards intelligible specificity, but also as regards the actual existence *(esse)* which it has in the nature of things. And it is in this mode that goodness is perfective; for the good is in things, as the Philosopher says in the text just referred to. Now, so far as one being is by its very act of existing perfective and conservative of another, it has the aspect of an end in respect to that which is perfected by it. And for this reason all who rightly define the good place in its definition something pertaining to the character of final causality. Accordingly, the Philosopher states in the first book of the *Ethics* that those defining the good in the most correct way declare it to be that which all desire (or aim at).[14]

Goodness, then, is primarily and principally predicated of being as perfective of another in the manner of an end. But a thing that is conducive to an end is said to be good derivatively—in the sense that the useful is said to be good. Or a thing is called good

12. *Secundum rationem speciei tantum.*
13. Cf. *Metaph.,* VI (E), 4 (1027b 25 f.).
14. Cf. *Eth. Nicom.,* I, 1 (1094a 3).

derivatively which is by its nature ordered to an end, as healthy is predicated not only of that which has health, but also of that which perfects and conserves and signifies health.[15]

Answers to Objections. 1. Since being *(ens)* is said absolutely, whereas goodness adds to being the relation of final causality, a thing's essence, absolutely considered, suffices for predicating being of it through that essence; but the essence does not suffice as a ground for predicating goodness of a thing, as it does in other genera of causes. The secondary cause depends on the first cause, but the first depends on no other. So it is in final causes, for the secondary ends participate in finality by their ordination to the ultimate end, while the latter enjoys this character—finality—in virtue of itself. And therefore God's essence, which is the ultimate end of things, suffices for this, that He be termed good in virtue of it. But in the case of the creature's essence, a thing is said to be good only in relation to God, from which relation it acquires the aspect of a final cause. And thus in one sense it is said that the creature is not good essentially, but participatively, namely, inasmuch as the created essence itself is considered as something other than the relation to God, whence it acquires the aspect of a final cause, and to Whom it is ordered as to an end. In another sense, however, the creature can be said to be good essentially, namely, inasmuch as the created essence does not in fact exist except in relation to the divine goodness. And this is the meaning Boethius has in mind there in the *De Hebdomadibus.*

2. Not only negation, but also a certain kind of relation, is said to be one of reason only, as is stated in the body of the Article.

3. Every real relation is in a determinate genus, but non-real relations can encompass all being.

4. Although diffusion, in the strict sense of the word, seems to imply the operation of an efficient cause, nevertheless, taken

15. E.g., exercise, food, and complexion are called good derivatively or secondarily inasmuch as they are, respectively, ordained to the end of perfecting, conserving, and signifying health in the living organism.

broadly, it can import reference to any kind of cause. . . . Now when it is said that the good is *diffusive* by its own nature, the term is not to be understood to imply the operation of an efficient cause—an effusion—but rather final causality; and the diffusion in question is not brought about through some superadded power. The word *good* expresses the diffusion of a final and not an efficient cause: both because the agent, as such, is not the measure and perfection of a thing, but rather its initiator, and because the effect participates in the efficient cause according to the assimilation of the form alone,[16] whereas a thing pursues its end according to its total being. And in this the nature of goodness consists.

5. Things can be really one in God in a twofold manner. *In one way,* exclusively in respect of that in which they exist, and not as regards their own nature. It is in this way that knowledge *(scientia)* and power, for example, are really one in God. For it is not by reason of its own nature that knowledge is the same in reality as power, but because the knowledge is in God. And things that are thus really one in God, are in creatures really diverse. *In another way,* certain things can be really one in God because it is their nature to be really one. Thus goodness and being are one in God really, because it pertains to the essence of goodness not to differ in reality from being; and therefore goodness and being are one in reality wherever they exist.

6. Just as there is a certain essential and a certain accidental being, so also in the case of goodness. And a thing loses its goodness, substantial or accidental, as it loses its being, substantial or accidental.

7. On account of the aforesaid relation [viz., to being as end or final cause] it happens that the good is said to determine or inform being according to reason [not in reality].

16. Isaac Israeli (Isaac Ben Salomon). On this classic definition, attributed to Isaac, see J. T. Muckle, C.S.B., "Isaac Israeli's Definition of Truth" (*Archives d'hist. doct. et litt. du moyen âge,* viii, 1933, pp. 5–8).

8. To this relation of reason between goodness and being something real does correspond, namely, the real dependence of that which is, with respect to the end itself; and so it is also with other relations of reason.

9. Although the word *good* does express a certain special relation, namely, that of final causality, nevertheless this relation belongs to every being, nor does it posit in the being anything real. Therefore the argument of the Objection does not follow.

10. Although *risible* is convertible with *man*, nevertheless it adds to man a certain nature over and above and extraneous to the essence of man. But, as was said, nothing can be added to being in this way.

Answers to Objections to the Contrary. 1. The first we concede, because goodness, as such, does not add a reality to being.

2. The second argument, however, concludes that goodness does not add anything to being according to reason, either. To this, then, it must be replied that a thing can be understood "without another" in two senses. *In one sense,* judgmentally,[17] namely, so long as one thing is understood to *exist* without the other. And in this sense, whatever the intellect can understand "without another," God can make. Now being cannot in this sense be understood "without" goodness, namely, so that some existing being is understood *not* to be good. *In another sense,* a thing can be understood "without another" after the manner of definition,[18] so that one thing is understood without including therein the concept or understanding of the other, as animal is understood "without" man, or any of its other species. And in this way, being can be understood "without" goodness.[19] Yet it does not follow that God can make

17. *De Veritate,* XI (PL 158, 480).
18. *Metaph.,* IV (Γ), 7 (1011b 25–29).
19. I.e., "being" signifies simply that which is or can be, and thus does not actually and explicitly include in its concept finality or conformity to appetite, signified by the term *good,* so that in this sense the meaning of the term *being* can be—indeed is—understood without understanding the meaning of the term *good.*

being "without" goodness, because the very act of making is the bringing forth of something into existence.

2. Are Being and Goodness Really the Same?[20]

Objections. 1. It seems that they are not. For opposites are by nature relative to the same thing. Now good and evil are opposites. Therefore, since evil is not by its nature fitted to be in all things (as Avicenna says,[21] "Beyond the circle of the moon there is no evil"), it seems that goodness likewise is not found in all beings, and thus that the good is not convertible with being.

2. Things so related that one of them is wider in extension than the other are not convertible. But, as the Commentator Maximus says in the fourth chapter of the *Divine Names*,[22] the term *good* extends to more things than *being* does; for good extends to non-existent entities [possibles] that are called forth into being by the good. Therefore goodness and being are not convertible.

3. Further, as Algazel says, the good is perfection, the apprehension of which causes delight. But not every being has perfection; for prime matter has no perfection whatever. Therefore not every being is good.

4. Further, being is found in mathematics, but not goodness, as is clear from what the Philosopher says in the third book of the *Metaphysics*.[23] Therefore goodness and being are not convertible.

---

20. *De Ver.*, XXI, 2. The question, translated literally, is: "Whether being and good are converted according to supposits?" This means: "Are they the same in their subjects?", and is equivalent to the question: "Are they really the same?" Cf. *ST* I, 5, 3: "Whether Every Being Is Good."

21. *Metaph.*, IX, cap. 6.

22. Cf. Boethius, *De Div. Nom.*, cap. 4. I have been unable to consult the commentary referred to.

23. *Metaph.*, III (B), 2 (996a 29).

5. Further, it is said in the *Book of Causes* that the first of created things is being.[24] Now, according to the Philosopher's statement in the *Categories*, that is prior whose consequent is not convertible with it.[25] Therefore the sequence from being to good is not reversible; that is to say, being and goodness are not convertible.

6. Further, a divided entity is not convertible with any of the things that divide it, just as animal is not convertible with rational. But being is divided by good and evil, since many entities are said to be evil. Therefore goodness and being are not convertible.

7. Further, according to the Philosopher, in the fourth book of the *Metaphysics,* privation is in a certain mode called a being.[26] But in no way can a privation be termed good; otherwise, evil, whose essence consists in privation, would be good. Therefore goodness and being are not convertible.

8. Further, according to Boethius, "it is for this reason that all things are said to be good, namely, because they are from the Good which is God."[27] But God's goodness is His wisdom and His justice. Consequently all things that are from God would be wise and just. Now this is false. Therefore, the first statement also is false, namely, that all things are good.

On the contrary, nothing tends to anything except its like. But every being tends toward goodness, as Boethius says.[28] Hence every being is good; nor can anything be good unless it in some way is. Therefore goodness and being are convertible.

Further, from the good nothing can follow except good. But every being proceeds from the divine Good. Therefore every being is good; and thus the conclusion is the same as that above.

24. *De Causis,* IV (p. 164).
25. Cf. *Categoriae,* 12 (14a 29).
26. Cf. *Metaph.,* IV (Γ), 2 (1003b 5 ff.).
27. *De Hebdom.* (PL 64, 1312).
28. *Loc. cit.*

I answer: Since the essence of goodness consists in this, that something be perfective of another in the manner of an end, every thing having the nature of an end, has also the nature of goodness. Two things, however, pertain to the nature of an end: 1) that it be sought after or desired by those things which have not yet attained it, and 2) that it be loved by, and as it were lovable to, those things which share in its possession; for it pertains to the same nature to tend toward its end, and in some way to rest in it, just as it is by one and the same nature that the stone is moved toward the center and rests there.[29] Now these two things [tendency and rest] belong to the very act of existing *(ipsum esse)*. For those things which do not yet have this act, tend toward it by a certain natural appetite. Thus matter, as the Philosopher says,[30] desires form. All things that presently have existence, however, naturally love that existence, and preserve it with all their power. So, in the third book of *The Consolation of Philosophy,*[31] Boethius says: "The divine providence gave to the things created by Him this special reason for remaining in existence, that to the extent of their capacity they would naturally desire to preserve their being. Wherefore you can in no way doubt this fact, that all things naturally desire the continuance of their existence and naturally shun their own destruction." The very act of existing *(ipsum esse)* thus has the character of goodness. Hence, just as it is impossible that there be any being which does not have this act, so it is necessary that every being be good precisely because it has this act; although in certain entities many aspects of goodness are superadded to the act of being whereby they subsist.

Now, since goodness includes the notion of being, as is clear from what has been said already, there could be no good which is not a being. It remains, therefore, that good and being are convertible.

29. Cf. Aristotle, *Phys.*, III, 5 (205b 16).
30. *Phys.*, I, 9 (192a 22).
31. *De Consol. Phil.*, *prosa* 11, *vers. fin.*

Answers to Objections. 1. Good and evil are opposed in the manner of a habitus and a privation, respectively. Yet it is not necessary that in whatever thing a habitus is present there should also naturally exist a privation. And so, whatever is by nature constituted to be good need not be constituted to be evil. In contraries, even when one of them is by nature present in something, the other one is not by its nature present in that same thing, as the Philosopher points out in the *Categories*.[32] But the goodness of each and every being is naturally present in it, since a being is called good in virtue of its own natural act of being.

2. Goodness does not extend to non-existent "entities" by predication, but by causality, inasmuch as they desire the good; so that we call "non-beings" those "beings" which are potentially and not actually existent. But the act of existing does not possess causality, unless it be under the aspect of an exemplar cause; and such a cause extends only to those things which have existence actually.

3. Just as prime matter is a being potentially, and not actually, so it is perfect potentially, and not actually, and good potentially, and not actually.

4. The objects which the mathematician considers are good as regards the existence *(esse)* they have in things. Thus the existence of a line or a number is itself good. Such entities, however, are not considered by the mathematician in their xistence, but only in their intelligible specificity. For the mathematician proceeds by way of abstraction, and mathematical entities are not abstract existentially, but only logically. It was said above, however, that goodness is not consequent upon intelligible specificity except according to the latter's existential realization in some thing. The character of goodness, then, does not pertain to the line or the number so far as they fall under

32. Cf. *Categoriae*, 10 (12a 10 ff.).

the mathematical mode of consideration, although lines and numbers *are* good.[33]

5. Being is not said to be prior to goodness in the sense implied by the Objection, but in another fashion, as the absolute is prior to what is related to it.[34]

6. A thing can be termed good, both in virtue of its own being, and of what is proper to its nature, or by some superadded relation. Thus a man is called good, both inasmuch as he is just and chaste, or because he is ordained to beatitude. By reason of the first goodness,[35] therefore, being is convertible with good, and vice versa; but by reason of the second,[36] good divides being.

7. Privation is not called a being of nature, but only a being of reason. And so it is a good of reason. For knowledge of privation, or of any such "entity," is good; and the knowledge of evil, as Boethius says, cannot lack goodness.

8. According to Boethius, a thing is said to be good in virtue of its own act of existing; but it is said to be just because of something pertaining to its action. Now the act of existing is poured forth into all things proceeding from God; yet not all things share that action to which justice is ordained. For, although in God acting is the same as existing, and in consequence. His justice *is* His goodness, nevertheless in creatures acting is one thing, existing another. So that the act of existing can be communicated to something to which action is not communicated; and in those things to which both are communicated, the acting is not the same as the existing. Thus, men who are good and just are indeed good so far as they are; yet they

---

33. Abstracted from existence and hence from goodness, mathematical entities, *qua* mathematical, are not "good"; but, *qua* entities—considered as existing in their real subjects—they are "good."

34. I.e., being is prior to goodness, not as entailing their non-convertibility, but in the sense that being expresses something absolutely, unqualifiedly, indeterminately, viz., that which is or can be, whereas good adds to being a certain relation.

35. Consequent upon the act of existing or subsisting.

36. The superadded relation.

are not just so far as they are, but so far as they possess a certain habitus ordained to action. And the same point applies in the case of wisdom and other such things.[37]

Or it must be said, regarding the same matter, that justice and wisdom and other things of the sort are certain special goods, since they are certain special perfections. The word *good*, however, designates something perfect, as such. From the perfection of God Himself perfect things proceed, but not in the same mode of perfection wherein God is perfect; because what comes to be does so, not according to the agent's mode of being, but according to that of the thing made. Nor do all things which receive perfection from God receive it in the same mode. And therefore, just as to be perfect[38] without further qualification is common to God and to all creatures, but not to be perfect in this or that mode, so it is also with goodness. For although goodness belongs to God and to all creatures, the possession of that goodness which is wisdom or justice need not be common to all. Rather, to God alone certain goods belong, such as eternity and omnipotence, while certain goods belong both to creatures and to God, such as wisdom, and justice, and the like.

¶ ARE ALL THINGS GOOD BY GOD'S GOODNESS?[39]

In things which entail relation, there is no reason why a thing cannot be denominated from something extrinsic to it. Thus a thing is denominated *placed* from place, and *measured* from measure. But as regards things that are called absolute, opinions differ. Plato held the separate existence of the essences of all things, and that individuals were denominated by them as participating in the separate essences; for instance, that Socrates is called man according to the separate

37. I.e., in the case of all perfections superadded to being that are found in the created order.
38. Actual, fulfilled.
39. *ST* I, 6, 4, c.

Idea (or Form) of man.[40] Now, just as he laid down separate Ideas of man and horse, which he called absolute *[per se]* man and absolute horse,[41] so likewise he posited separate Ideas of *being* and of *one,* which he called absolute being and absolute oneness;[42] and by participation in these everything was called being or one. What was thus absolute being and absolute unity, he said was the highest good.[43] And because *good* is convertible *being,* as is also *one,* he called the absolute good God,[44] from whom all things are called good by way of participation.[45]

Although this opinion appears to be unreasonable in maintaining that there are separate forms of natural things subsisting of themselves—as Aristotle argues in many ways—[46] nevertheless it is absolutely true that there is something first which is being and good in virtue of its own essence, namely, He whom we call God, as is clear from what was proved above. . . .[47]

Everything is therefore called good from God's goodness, as from the first exemplar, efficient, and final principle of all goodness. Nevertheless, everything is called good by reason of the likeness of God's goodness inhering in it, which likeness is its own goodness whereby it is denominated good. And so of all things there is one Goodness, and yet many goodnesses.

40. Cf. Aristotle, *Metaph.,* I (A), 6 (987b 7).
41. Aristotle, *Metaph.,* III (B), 2 (997b 8).
42. *Op. cit.,* III (B), 4 (999b 26).
43. Cf. Aristotle, *Eth. Nicom.,* I, 6 (1096a 23).
44. St. Augustine, *De Civit. Dei,* VIII, 8 (PL 41, 233); cf. Plato, *Republic,* VI (508 C).
45. Cf. St. Augustine, *De Trin.,* VIII, 3 (PL 42, 949).
46. E.g., in *Metaph.,* I (A), 9 (990a 33); VI (E), 7–8; *Eth. Nicom.,* I, 6 (1096a 11).
47. Q. 4, a. 3.

IX

THE TRANSCENDENTAL: *BEAUTY*

1. INTRODUCTORY

NOTHING EXISTS which does not participate in beauty and goodness, since each thing is beautiful and good according to its proper form. . . . Created beauty is nothing other than a likeness of the divine beauty participated in things.[1]

Now[2] beauty and goodness are the same in subject because they are based upon the same reality, the form. And for this reason goodness is praised as beautiful. Yet they differ in reason. For the good properly regards the opposite (the good being what all desire), and thus it has the character of an end, seeing that appetite is a certain motion toward a thing. Beauty, on the other hand, regards the cognitive power, because those things are said to be beautiful which please when seen. Beauty accordingly consists in due proportion, for sense delights in things rightly proportioned, as in things like unto itself; indeed sense itself is a kind of reason, as every cognitive

---

1. *De Div. Nom.*, IV, 5 *(ad finem)*.
2. *ST* I, 5, 4, ad 1.

power is. And because cognition is effected through assimilation, and assimilation concerns the form, beauty properly pertains to the nature of a formal cause.[3]

For beauty three things are required: a) integrity or perfection, b) right proportion or consonance, c) splendor of form.[4]

3. Since being and goodness are convertible, so also are being and beauty. And just as goodness differs from being only in reason, so does beauty differ from being only in reason. It is not to be inferred from the text cited above that for St. Thomas beauty is limited to the order of sense knowledge or experience. Nor is the famous statement—"those things are said to be beautiful which when seen please"—to be taken as a formal, analytical definition of beauty, but simply as a nominal, descriptive one, as the context indeed makes clear. Cf.: "Pulchrum *dicatur* id cujus ipsa apprehensio placet." *ST* I-II, 27, 1, and 3.

4. *ST* I, 39, 8 *(med.)*. Regarding these important requirements allow me to note the following, in order: a) *"Integritas* [organic wholeness, interior unity] is consequent upon perfection, which consists in a thing's very act of existing." (*In IV Sent.,* XXVI, 2, 4.) b) *Debita proportio sive consonatia* signifies the order and harmony whereby things are fittingly related to each other and, primarily, are directed to God. "Consonance in things is twofold: one as regards the ordination of creatures to God [as their last end or good], the other [secondary one] as regards the ordering of things to one another." (*De Div. Nom.,* IV, 5.) c) *Claritas,* a word which seems to be untranslatable literally, includes the notion of intelligibility, since it means the cognitive—and not only intellectual—manifestness of the thing's form. From this statement of the formal requirements of beauty it can be seen that beauty synthesizes in a certain way, or embraces, being, goodness, and truth. Integrity and perfection pertain to being, existence, and unity; proportion or consonance to order, finality, and thus to goodness; splendor of form *(claritas)* to intelligibility and hence to truth. (For a thorough textual study concluding with this capital point, see Rev. Gerald B. Phelan: "The Concept of Beauty in St. Thomas Aquinas," in *Some Aspects of the New Scholastic Philosophy,* Benziger Bros., 1932; pp. 121–145.) It may be said that truth and beauty differ formally in this: whereas truth lies in the conformity of being, *qua* intelligible, and intellect, beauty consists in the conformity of being, *qua* "consonant" in the sense defined, and cognitive power in general of intelligent beings—a conformity resulting not in merely apprehending that which is, but also in loving and resting in it. (Cf. *De Div. Nom.,* IV, 5, 6.)

2. On Beauty and the Divine Beauty[5]

God, Who is "supersubstantially beautiful, is called Beauty," as Dionysius says, because He confers beauty upon all created beings according to the peculiar nature of each one. . . . God bestows beauty inasmuch as He is "the cause of harmony *(consonantia)* and splendor of form *(claritas)* in all things." For we say a man is beautiful by reason of the seemly proportion, in quantity and position, of his members, and therefore we declare that he has a distinguished and splendid appearance. This notion, then, is to be applied analogously *(proportionaliter)* in all other contexts, so that every thing will be called "beautiful" according to its own kind of luminousness *(claritas),* whether spiritual or corporeal, and according as it is disposed in due proportion *(debita proportione).*

Now Dionysius shows how God is the cause of splendor of form, saying that He transmits to all creatures, with a certain lightning-like brightness, a ray of His own brilliant light, which is the source of all illumination. And these lightning-like communications of the divine ray of light are to be understood according to analogical

5. The following two sections comprise almost the whole of Lectures 5 and 6, Chapter IV of the Thomas Commentary on *The Divine Names (De Divinis Nominibus)* of the Pseudo-Dionysius. Here we find the most extensive presentation of *St. Thomas'* doctrine of beauty. For the Angelic Doctor, in appropriating the thought of the Pseudo-Dionysius, interprets it in the light of his own metaphysics. The properly Platonic or neo-Platonic *philosophical* overtones and implications of the Pseudo-Dionysian text (profoundly Christian though it is) are absent from St. Thomas' Commentary. Thus one will note in the latter the orientation toward *esse,* as act of existing; the consequent existential analogicity of being *qua* beautiful and of its participation and its causality. That is to say, St. Thomas' Commentary is far from being a simple exposition of the Pseudo-Dionysius' own thought on beauty; the words in which the latter is expressed are accepted whole-heartedly by St. Thomas, but their precise *metaphysical* meaning in the Pseudo-Dionysius is not formally the same metaphysical meaning attributed to them by St. Thomas—though their specifically Christian import, of course, is substantially identical in the minds of both these Christian thinkers.

participation; and as Dionysius says, they are "beautifying," that is, productive of beauty in things.

Regarding the other point made by Dionysius, namely, that God is the cause of harmony (*consonantia*—order and proportion) in things, we must note that this harmony is twofold. First, there is the harmony that consists in the ordination of creatures to God. And here Dionysius says God is the cause of harmony "as summoning all things to Himself," in that He converts all things to Himself as their end. . . . And for this reason beauty in Greek is καλὸς, a word derived from the act of calling [καλέω]. The second harmony in things, however, lies in their ordination to each other. And this Dionysius refers to when he says that God unites all with all in relation to the same. Superiors, indeed, as the Platonists held, are in inferiors by participation, whereas inferiors are in superiors by a certain excellence, or transcendence; so that all things *are* in all things. And from the fact that all are in all in a certain order, it follows that all are ordered to the same end.

Beauty, as Dionysius shows, is predicated of God by way of excess, or transcendence. Excess, however, is two-fold: the one generic, which is signified by the comparative or the superlative; the other extra-generic, which is signified by the addition of the preposition *super*. For instance, if we say fire "exceeds" in heat generically, then fire is spoken of as "most hot." The sun, on the other hand, "exceeds" extra-generically; so it is not said to be "most hot," but "super-hot," because heat is not in the sun in the same mode as in fire, but in a higher mode. Although this twofold excess is not simultaneously present in caused things, nevertheless God is said to be at once "most beautiful" and "super-beautiful": not that He is in a genus, but that all things of whatever genus are attributed [analogically] to Him. . . .

Now, just as a thing is said to be "more white" because it is less mixed with black, so a thing is said to be "more beautiful" in proportion to its immunity from any defect of beauty. But in creatures there is a twofold defect of beauty. *One* consists in the fact that some things exist whose beauty is variable, as is evidently the case with corruptible things. This defect Dionysius excludes from God first of all, saying that God is beautiful always, in the same respect and the same mode, any alteration of beauty being foreign to Him. Moreover, there is in God neither generation nor corruption of beauty, nor any change, either of increase or diminution, as is manifestly true of corporeal things. Now *the second defect of beauty* lies in this: all creatures have beauty that is in some way particularized, just as they have a particularized nature. This defect Dionysius excludes from God as regards every mode of particularity. God, he says, is not in one part beautiful and in another ugly, as happens sometimes in particular things; nor is God beautiful at one time and at another not, as are things whose beauty is subject to time; nor is He beautiful in one relation and not in another, as with all things ordained to one determinate use or end (for, were they directed to something else, harmony would not be served, and hence neither would beauty); nor, again, is God in one place beautiful and in another not, as some things are because they seem beautiful to certain persons and to others not. On the contrary, God is absolutely and in every way beautiful. And Dionysius gives the explanation of all this by saying God is beautiful "according to Himself." For this phrase eliminates any possibility that He is beautiful in one respect only, or in a certain time only, or in a certain place only, because what belongs to a being "according to itself," or in virtue of its own being, and does so primarily, belongs to it totally and everlastingly and ubiquitously. Further, God is beautiful in Himself, not in respect to something determinate, or limited; so that it cannot be said He is beautiful in one regard and in another, not. . . . Finally, God is always and uniformly beautiful; and thus is excluded from Him the first defect of beauty, namely, variability.

Dionysius shows further why God is called "superbeautiful," namely, because He possesses in Himself eminently, and prior to all other beings, the source of all beauty. In God, the simple and supernatural Essence of all beautiful things derived from Him, every beauty and every beautiful being pre-exists, not indeed dividedly, but uniformly [unitedly and simply], in the manner in which multiple effects pre-exist in their cause.

3. THE CAUSALITY OF BEAUTY[6]

Dionysius points out that from this divine Beauty, existence (*esse*) comes to all existing beings. Now, as was said, splendor of form (*claritas*) pertains to the consideration of beauty. But every form, through which a thing has actual existence, is a certain participation of the divine intelligible Splendor (*divina claritas*). And so Dionysius adds: "singular things are beautiful according to their proper intelligible essence (*ratio*)"; and this means, according to their proper form. It is therefore evident that the act of existing (*esse*) of all things stems from the divine Beauty. It was noted, moreover, that harmony (*consonantia*) is intrinsic to the essence of beauty. Hence all things which in any way appertain to harmony [and thus to order and proportion] proceed from the divine Beauty. Dionysius thus states that it is because of the divine Beauty that there are "harmonious relationships" (*concordiae*), as regards understanding, among all rational creatures (for those are in accord with each other whose thought is one), and "friendships" (*amicitiae*), as regards affection, and "fellowships" (*communiones*), as regards action, or something extrinsic; and universally, all creatures, whatsoever unity they may have among themselves, possess that unity in virtue of the beautiful.

Dionysius goes on to say, in the first place, that "the beautiful is the principle of all things as their effective cause," bestowing being upon them, and as their "moving cause," and as the "containing (that is, conserving) cause of all things." Now these three

---

6. Continuation: *op. cit.*, IV, 5.

offices seem to pertain to the efficient cause, namely, to give existence *(esse)*, to move, and to conserve. But there is a certain kind of efficient cause that acts out of desire for an end, and such action is proper to an imperfect agent, one which does not yet possess what is desires, or tends toward. On the contrary, it pertains to the perfect agent to act out of love of that which it possesses. And for this reason, Dionysius adds that the Beauty which is God is the effective, motive, and containing Cause "through love of His own beauty." For since God possesses beauty, He wishes to multiply it so far as that is possible, namely, by communication of its likeness. Secondly, Dionysius says that the Beauty which is God is "the end of all things, as final cause" of all things. For it is in order to imitate, in whatsoever manner, the divine Beauty that all things are made. Thirdly, the divine Beauty is the exemplar cause, since it is by reference to the divine Beauty that all things are distinguished, and the sign of this is that no one cares to portray or represent anything except in accordance with his idea of beauty *(nisi ad pulchrum)*.

Finally, when Dionysius avers, "On this account, too, the beautiful is the same as the good," he draws a certain corollary from what he had said, remarking that because the beautiful is the cause of all things in all these ways, it follows that the good and the beautiful are the same. For indeed all things desire the beautiful and the good in all these modes, and there is nothing that does not participate in beauty and goodness, since each thing is beautiful and good according to its proper form. Moreover, we can even declare boldly with Dionysius that "the non-existent," that is to say, prime matter, "participates in beauty and goodness," inasmuch as this non-actual primal "being" has a certain likeness to the divine beauty and goodness. For beauty and goodness in God are extolled through the exclusion of all imperfections or limitations. In the case of prime matter it is indeed a question of exclusion by way of defect; in God, of exclusion by way of excess, seeing that God exists super-substantially.

However, although beauty and goodness are the same in reality—for both splendor of form *(claritas)* and harmony *(consonantia)* are contained in the notion of goodness—nevertheless, they differ in reason, because beauty adds to goodness ordination to cognitive power.[7]

Now[8] Dionysius explains that although goodness and beauty are one in their very being *(unum esse),* they are the "cause of all goods and beauties"—which are many. . . . He points out that beauty is the cause of the substantial essences of things. For every essence is either a simple form,[9] or has its substantial completion through its substantial form. But a form is a certain irradiation from the Primary Splendor of Form.[10] And, as was said, splendor of form pertains to the essence of beauty.

Again, in speaking of "unities and distinctions," Dionysius notes the things that pertain to the concept of unity. And what we must consider here is that *one* adds to the notion of being, indivision; for *one* means undivided being. Thus, opposed to unity is distinction or division. Now the cause of the "unities and distinctions" of things, Dionysius declares, is the divine Beauty. Let us recall that oneness in substance is the cause of identity; distinctness in substance, the cause of diversity, . . , while similarity is caused by oneness in quality. . . . It is an evident fact, moreover, that dissimilar entities agree in something (e.g., contraries agree in genus and in matter, or subject), and that things united accidentally remain distinct as parts in their whole. (Respecting the first of these Dionysius uses the expression "communions of contraries," and for the second "intermixtures of units.") Now the point is this: all these things are reduced to the causality of the beautiful, because they appertain to harmony *(consonantia*—order, proportion), which in turn is of the essence of beauty, as was said above.

7. End, *op. cit.,* IV, 5.
8. *Op. cit.,* IV, 6.
9. As the angel is.
10. *Prima claritas,* viz., God.

Further, speaking of the "providence of superiors," Dionysius enumerates that which pertains to the order of things. And first he considers this problem from the standpoint of action—according as superiors provide for inferiors (he touches upon this in referring to "the reciprocal relations of coordinate things," that is, of equals), and also according as inferiors are ordained to the reception from superiors of perfection and governance. . . .

Secondly, he notes what pertains to the existence of things in themselves, declaring that the perdurances whereby certain things (that is, things-in-themselves) are kept in being have their principle in the beautiful. For a thing is kept in existence by the fact that it remains within the limits of its nature, since if it so to speak poured itself out altogether, it would perish. And Dionysius adds the phrase: "And dissimilar collocations," that is, foundations. For, just as a thing is conserved in being by remaining in itself, so is it intransmutable by having something intrinsically solid upon which it is founded.

Thirdly, Dionysius cites the things that pertain to the abiding presence of one thing in another. It must be borne in mind, he points out, that when something is to be constructed from a number of other things, the *prime requisite* is that the parts be in conformity. For instance, the stones of which a house is built are by nature conformed to each other. Similarly, all the parts of the universe come together and form a unity in virtue of their common act of existing. Dionysius therefore says that not only the abiding presence of things in themselves has its source in the beautiful, but also the "communions of all things in all things according to the proper nature of each." For it is not in one mode that all things are in all things; rather, superiors are in inferiors by participation; inferiors in superiors excellently.[11] Yet all share something in common with all.

---

11. I.e., in a higher mode than they are in themselves.

Moreover, for something to be constituted by a number of things, it is necessary, *secondly*, that they be adaptable to one another even as regards that in which they are diverse. Thus a house would not be made of cement and stone unless these things were fitted to exist together. Likewise the parts of the universe are adapted to each other inasmuch as they can fall under one order.[12]

The *third requirement* is that the one part be served by the other. Thus the walls and the roof of a building are supported by the foundation, and the roof completely covers the walls and the foundation. So, too, in the universe higher things give perfection to lower things, and in the lower thing a higher power is manifested. Hence Dionysius' phrase: "and friendships not disordered"; for relations of mutual service among things are not prejudicial to their distinctness.

A *fourth requirement* is due proportion in the parts. The foundation, for example, must be proportioned to the other parts. Therefore Dionysius adds: "and the harmony of the whole," that is, of all the parts of the universe. Thus harmony is caused in sounds by the right proportion of numbers. Therefore, the parts having been thus disposed,[13] their unification in the whole follows, so that from all the parts of the universe one totality *(universitas)* of things is constituted. . . .

This "concretion" of parts in the universe is attained in two ways. First, by means of that "local" containment whereby superiors in some fashion are in things in place of inferiors, whether spiritual or corporeal. Hence Dionysius' phrase: "indissoluble containments of existing things"; that is to say, superiors contain inferiors in an indissoluble order. Secondly, this concretion of parts in the universal whole is attained as regards the succession of time, so far as generable and corruptible things (wherein the posterior succeed the prior) are concerned. Consequently, Dionysius appends

---

12. Thereby forming a single system or whole.
13. I.e., harmoniously ordered.

this expression: "the unfailing successions of the things that are made." The successions of things indeed are said to be "unfailing," not because genera endure forever, but because some succeed others without interruption as long as this world process *(cursus mundi)* lasts. Now all these things, as Dionysius says, are caused by beauty, because they pertain to the nature of harmony *(consonantia)*, which in turn is of the essence of beauty.

Further, Dionysius says that "all rests and motions," inasmuch as they import some relation of one thing to another, belong to the notion of harmony and beauty. . . . Indeed he declares that all rests and motions, whether of souls or of bodies, are caused by the divine Beauty. And he says this because . . . that which is above all rest and motion is the cause of both rest and motion in all things, inasmuch as it establishes each thing in its proper nature, wherein the thing has its resting place [so to speak], and inasmuch as it moves all things in relation to the divine motion. For the motions of all things are ordered to the motion whereby they are moved toward God, as the motions relative to secondary ends are ordered to the motion which is directed to the ultimate end. Now the form upon which the proper nature of a thing depends, pertains to intelligible splendor *(claritas)*, and order to the end [finality] pertains to harmony *(consonantia)*. Therefore motion and rest are reduced to the causality of the beautiful.[14]

14. End, *op. cit.,* IV, 6. Some slight paraphrasing has seemed necessary in order to render the foregoing into clear English.

X

METAPHYSICS AS *SCIENTIA DIVINA*

1. Does Divine Science Treat of Those Things that Exist Without Matter and Motion?[1]

T seems that divine science does not treat of things separated from motion and matter.

Objections. 1. Apparently divine science is, above all, about God. But we cannot attain to a knowledge of God except through visible effects, which are rooted in matter and motion. Rom. 1:20: "The invisible things of Him from the creation of the world are clearly seen, being understood by the things that are made." Therefore divine science does not abstract from matter and motion.

2. That to which motion in any manner appertains is not altogether separated from matter and motion. But motion in some way appertains to God: wherefore it is said of the divine wisdom (Wisd. 7:22, 24) that it is active and more active than all active things. And Augustine says[2] that God moves Himself without time and place; and Plato held[3] that the first mover moves himself.

---

1. *In Boeth. de Trin.*, V, 4.
2. *De Genesi ad litteram*, VIII, n 39 (PL 34, 388).
3. Cf. *Phaedrus*, 245 D.

Therefore divine science, which treats of God, is not altogether separated from motion.

3. The study not only of God but also of the angels falls within the province of divine science. But the angels are moved both according to choice (since from being good they became bad) and according to place, as is clear in regard to those who have been sent as messengers. Therefore the things that divine science considers are not altogether separated from motion.

4. As the Commentator seems to say in the beginning of his *Physics*,[4] all that is, is either pure matter or pure form or a composite of matter and form. But an angel is not a pure form; if it were, it would be pure act, which only God is. Nor is the angel pure matter. Therefore it is composed of matter and form. It follows that divine science does not abstract from matter.

5. Divine science, which is held to be the third part of speculative philosophy, is the same as metaphysics, whose subject is being, and especially that being which is substance, as is clearly stated in the fourth book of the *Metaphysics*.[5] But being and substance do not abstract from matter; otherwise no being which had matter would be found in existence. Therefore divine science does not abstract from matter.

6. According to the Philosopher in the first book of the *Posterior Analytics*,[6] it is the office of a science to consider not only its subject but also the parts and passions of that subject. But being is the subject of divine science, as has been said. Thus it pertains to divine science to consider all beings. But matter and motion are beings in a certain sense, and thus the study of them belongs to metaphysics. So it is that divine science does not abstract from matter and motion.

4. Averroes, *In I Physicae,* com. 1 (Venetiis 1574, fol. 6ʳ).
5. Aristotle, *Metaph.,* IV (Γ), 1 (1003a 21); 2 (1003b 17 f.).
6. *Anal. Post.,* I, 28 (87a 38 f.).

7. As the Commentator says in the first book of his *Physics*,[7] divine science demonstrates by means of three causes: the efficient, the formal and the final. But the *efficient* cause cannot be taken into account without considering motion; likewise, neither can the *final* cause, as is stated in the third book of the *Metaphysics*.[8] Hence in mathematics, because its objects are immobile, no demonstration is made through causes of these two kinds. Therefore divine science does not abstract from motion.

8. Theology treats of the creation of heaven and earth and the acts of men, and many such things which in themselves contain matter and motion. Therefore theology seems not to abstract from matter and motion.

On the contrary, we have the Philosopher's statement in the sixth book of the *Metaphysics*,[9] that first philosophy is concerned with beings separable from matter and with things immobile. But first philosophy is divine science, as he says there also.[10] Therefore divine science is abstracted from matter and motion.

Moreover, the noblest science is about the noblest things. But divine science is the noblest science. Immaterial and immobile things being the noblest of all, it follows that divine science will treat of them.

I answer: It must be said that to make clear what this question means it is necessary to know which of the sciences ought to be called "divine science." Bear in mind, then, that whatever science considers a certain genus [or order of being] as its subject must consider the principles of that genus, since science is not fulfilled except through knowledge of principles, as the Philosopher states in the beginning of the *Physics*.[11] But there are two kinds of principles:

7. Averroes, *loc. cit.*
8. Cf. Aristotle, *Metaph.*, III (B), 2 (996a 22-27).
9. Cf. *Metaph.*, VI (E), 1 (1026a 16).
10. *Ibid.*, lines 19-21.
11. *Phys.*, I, 1 (184a 10-12).

1) Those which are in themselves complete natures and yet are also principles of other things. (Thus the celestial bodies are in a certain way principles of other inferior bodies; and simple bodies, of mixed bodies.) Such things then are considered, in the sciences treating of them, not only as principles but also as realities in themselves. And for this reason not only are they dealt with in that science which considers them as principiates, but they have also a distinct science of their own. For instance, there is a certain branch of natural science that deals with heavenly bodies, distinct from that branch in which inferior bodies are considered, and a branch that treats of the elements, distinct from the one concerned with mixed bodies. 2) There are certain other principles, however, that are not complete natures in themselves but are only principles of natures, as unity is in relation to number, a point with respect to a line, and form and matter as regards a physical body. Hence principles of this kind are dealt with only in that science which treats of the things flowing from those principles.

Now, just as there are certain common principles belonging to every determinate genus and extending to all the principles of that genus, so too all beings, as regards their common participation in being, have certain principles that are the principles of all beings. These principles indeed can be called "common" in two ways, as Avicenna says in his *Sufficientia*.[12] In one way, by predication, as when I say that "form is common to all forms" because it is predicated of any form whatever; in another way, by causality, as when we say that numerically one and the same sun is the principle of all generable things. Now of all beings there are principles common not only according to this first mode (which the Philosopher in the twelfth book of the *Metaphysics*[13] calls having the same principles "according to analogy"), but also according to the second mode, there being certain things numerically the same which are the

12. *Sufficientia*, I, 2 (Venetiis 1508, fol. 14ᵛa).
13. *Metaph.*, XII (Λ), 4 (1070a 31 f.).

principles of all things. So, for example, principles of accidents are reduced to principles of substance, and principles of corruptible things to incorruptible substances. Thus all things, in a certain grade and order, are reduced to various principles. And since that which is the principle of existence for all beings must needs be being in the highest mode, as is said in the second book of the *Metaphysics*,[14] principles of this [ultimate] kind must be in the highest degree complete, and hence most perfectly actual, having nothing, or the very least, of potentiality, because (as shown in the ninth book of the *Metaphysics*[15]) act is prior to and more powerful than potentiality. These principles therefore must be without matter, which is in potentiality, and without motion, which is the act of a thing existing in potentiality. Of such an order are divine things; for if the divine exists anywhere it exists above all in such a nature, namely, an immaterial and immobile one, as is stated in the sixth book of the *Metaphysics*.[16]

Thus, because they are principles of all beings and yet are natures complete in themselves, divine things can be considered in two ways: in one way as the common principles of all beings, in another as realities in themselves. However, as Aristotle remarks in the second book of the *Metaphysics*,[17] principles of this kind, though supremely intelligible in themselves, are in relation to our intellect as the light of the sun to the eyes of the owl; so that we cannot by the light of natural reason attain to them except as we are led to them through their effects. And in this way the philosophers arrived at a knowledge of them, according to Rom. 1:20: "The invisible things of God are clearly seen, being understood through the things that are made." Therefore such divine things are dealt with by philosophers only so far as they are principles of all things, and hence they are studied in that doctrine wherein the principles

14. *Metaph.*, II (α), 1 (993b 24-31).
15. *Metaph.*, IX (H), 8 (1049b 5); 9 (1051a4f.).
16. *Metaph.*, VI (E), 1 (1026a 20).
17. *Metaph.*, II (α), 1 (993b 9-11).

common to all beings are established and whose subject is being as being; and among the philosophers this science is called "divine science." There is however another way of knowing divine things, not as they are made manifest through their effects, but according as they manifest themselves. This way of knowing divine things the Apostle speaks of in I Cor. 2:11 f.: "The things also that are of God no man knoweth, but the Spirit of God. Now we have received not the spirit of this world, but the Spirit that is of God"; and (2:10): "To us God hath revealed them, by His Spirit." And in this way divine things are considered according as they subsist in themselves, and not only so far as they are principles of things.

Thus theology or divine science is twofold: *one* in which divine things are considered not so much as the subject of the science but as the principles of its subject, and such is that theology which the philosophers sought after and which by another name is called "metaphysics"; the *other* which considers divine things on their own account as the very subject of its science, and this is that theology which is communicated in Sacred Scripture. Both theologies, however, are concerned with things existing apart from matter and motion, but in diverse ways, according as a thing can exist in separation from matter and motion in either of two ways: in *one* way if by reason of its very nature it can in no wise exist in union with matter and motion, and thus are God and the angels said to be "separated" from matter and motion; in *another way* if the thing is not by its very nature existent in matter and motion but can exist apart therefrom, though it may sometimes be found in matter and motion; and thus being and substance, potency and act, are "separated" from matter and motion, because they do not depend upon matter and motion for their existence, as do mathematical objects, which can never exist except in matter, although they can be understood without sensible matter. Philosophical theology therefore treats as its subjects things separated in the second way, but things separated in the first way it deals with as principles of its subject. The theology of Sacred Scripture, on the other hand, treats as its subjects things separated in the first way, although in this science some things existing in matter and motion are dealt with, as the manifestation of divine things requires.

Answers to Objections. 1. Things introduced into a science only in order to bring to light other matters do not pertain to that science essentially but only as it were accidentally. So it is that mathematics of various kinds are employed in the field of natural science. Thus there is no reason why certain things implicated in matter and motion should not be dealt with [per accidens] in divine science.

2. Movement cannot be predicated of God properly but only as it were metaphorically, and this in a twofold manner. In *one way* according as the operation of the intellect or of the will is termed, improperly, a motion, so that a person is said to "move" himself when he knows or loves himself. And taken in this way Plato's dictum can be verified, for Plato said[18] that the first mover moves himself, since indeed he knows and loves himself, as the Commentator remarks, writing on the eighth book of Aristotle's *Physics*.[19] In *another way* according as the efflux of effects from their causes can be called a procession or a kind of motion of the cause into the effect, since in the effect itself there is left a likeness of the cause, so that the cause, which at first existed in itself, afterward is in its effect by its own likeness. And in this way God, Who confers a likeness of Himself upon all creatures, is in a certain [metaphorical] sense said to move through all things or to proceed to all things. This manner of speaking Dionysius frequently employs.[20] And apparently it is in accordance with this usage that we must understand what is said is Wisd. 7:24: "Wisdom is more active than all active things, and reacheth mightily from end

---

18. *Phaedrus*, 245 D; *Laws*, X, 895 B.
19. Averroes, *In VIII Physicae*, com. 40 (Venetiis 1574, VI, fol. 380ʳ).
20. Cf. Pseudo-Dionysius, *De divinis nominibus*, IX, 9 (PG 3, 916C).

to end." Now this activity of the Divine Wisdom is not movement properly so called. Therefore the conclusion of the Objection does not follow.

3. The divine science which has been received through Divine inspiration does not deal with the angels as its subject but only as things taken up in order to make manifest that subject. Thus in Sacred Scripture the angels are treated of just as other creatures are also. But in that divine science which the philosophers teach, the angels (whom they call intelligences) are considered under the same formal aspect [that of real causal principle] as is the first cause, God. That is to say, the angels are here treated as second principles of things, at least so far as the motion of the spheres is concerned, although no physical motion can be attributed to the angels.[21] Moreover, the "motion" involved in choice is reduced to the same kind as that attributed to the act of the intellect or the will, namely, motion improperly so called-motion taken for operation. Then too, the motion whereby the angels are said to move locally is not motion in respect of circumscribed place, but of the operation they exercise in this or that place; or it is motion as regards some other relation which they have to a place, a relation utterly diverse (omnino aequivocam) from that which a body in place has to place. Hence it is evident that "motion" in reference to the angels has nothing in common with the motion by which physical bodies are said to be in motion.

4. Act and potentiality are principles more common than matter and form. Therefore, although no composition of matter and form exists in the angels, there can be found in them potentiality and act. For matter and form are the parts of a thing composed of matter and form; hence in such things only is a composition of matter and form present, the matter being related

---

21. In metaphysics, God, in common with the angels, is considered as an immaterial, immobile principle or cause of real being, although He is so in an analogical mode infinitely transcending that of any angel.

to the form as potentiality to act. But what is able to be is able also not to be. Therefore one part can be found with the other and without the other, and for this reason a composition of matter and form is found, according to the Commentator,[22] solely in things corruptible by nature. Nor is this inconsistent with the abiding presence of some accident or other in some perpetually existent subject, as the accident of figure in the heavens, since after all the celestial body could not exist without such an accident. For figure and all the other accidents follow from the substance as from their cause. The subject is thus related to its accidents not only as a passive potency but also in a certain manner as an active one, so that some accidents naturally exist perpetually in their subjects. However, matter is not in this way the cause of form, and therefore every matter which is the subject of a form can also not be its subject, unless perchance it be maintained [as its subject] by an extrinsic cause. Thus we hold that it is by the divine power that some bodies, though composed of contrary elements, are incorruptible, such as the bodies of those risen from the dead. But since the angelic essence is by its very nature incorruptible, there is in it no composition of matter and form. Yet, because the angel does not have existence from itself, it is in potency to the existence which it receives from God; and its existence received from God is related to its simple essence as act to potentiality. And this is what is meant by the statement that angels are composed of *quod est* and of *quo est*, the very act of existing being understood by the *quo est* and the angelic nature by the *quod est*. If, however, the angels were composed of matter and form, this could not be sensible matter, from which mathematical entities must be abstracted and metaphysical ones separated.

5. Being and substance are said to be separated from matter and motion, not by reason of the fact that it is of their nature to be

22. Averroes, *In I De Coelo,* com. 20 (Venetiis 1574, VII, fol. 15ʳ]); *In VIII Metaph.,* com. 4 (Venetiis 1574, X, fol. 211ʳ, com. 12, fol. 220ʳ).

without matter and motion, as it is the nature of an ass to be without reason, but because it is not required by their nature that they be in matter and motion, although sometimes they are in matter and motion. For instance, the term "animal" abstracts from rationality, and yet some animal is rational.

6. The metaphysician considers even singular beings, not indeed according to their proper intelligible natures whereby they are beings of such and such a kind, but according as they participate in the common intelligible object which is being. And so it is that matter and motion also fall within the metaphysician's purview.

7. To act and to be acted upon do not pertain to beings according to their presence in thought, but as they are in existence. The mathematician, however, considers abstract things according to their presence in thought only; so that these things, so far as they come under his consideration, cannot be the principle or the end of motion. And it is for this reason that the mathematician makes no demonstrations through efficient and final causes. But realities that the theologian [or the metaphysician] considers are things separated [from matter and motion] and actually existing in the real world; and as such they can be the principle and end or final cause of motion. Nothing, then, prevents him from demonstrating through efficient and final causes.

8. Faith, which is as it were the habitus of the principles of theology, has the First Truth as its object, yet certain other things pertaining to creatures are contained in the articles of faith so far as they are in some way related to the First Truth. So likewise theology has God principally as its subject, but it also treats extensively of creatures as His effects, or as being related to Him in any way whatever.

2. On the Procedure Proper to Divine Science[23]

Just as to proceed by way of ratiocination is attributed to natural philosophy because in it the mode of reason[24] is especially observed, so to proceed by way of intellection is attributed to divine science since in it the mode of intellect[25] is especially observed. Now reason differs from intellect as multitude from unity. Hence Boethius says in *The Consolation of Philosophy*[26] that the relation of reason to intellect is similar to that of time to eternity and of the circle to its center. For it is proper to reason to be spread abroad, as it were, over many things, and from them to acquire one simple cognition. Hence in the seventh chapter of *The Divine Names*[27] Dionysius says that souls, according as they have the power of ratiocination, encompass the truth in a roundabout way, and in this respect are inferior to the angels, though inasmuch as they resolve the many into the one, they are in a certain manner equal to the angels.

Intellect, on the other hand, considers first of all the one and simple truth, and in it grasps its knowledge of the whole multiplicity, just as God in knowing His essence is cognizant of all things. Wherefore Dionysius says in the same place that the minds of the angels possess intellectuality inasmuch as they apprehend uniformly the intelligible essences of divine things.

It is therefore evident that the rational consideration[28] finds its termination in the intellectual[29] by way of resolution, inasmuch as from many things the reason gathers the one and simple truth. And again, intellectual consideration is the principle of the rational by way of composition and discovery, inasmuch as intellect grasps many things in one. Therefore that consideration which is the terminus of all human ratiocination is above all the intellectual. But the entire consideration of reason in its resolutive

23. Response to the Third Part, *In Boeth. de Trin.*, VI, 1.
24. *Modus rationis*, i.e., the process of rational discourse.
25. *Modus intellectus*, i.e., intellectual intuition.
26. *De consol. phil.*, IV, prosa 6.
27. *De div. nom.*, VII, 2 (PG 3, 868BC).
28. *Rationalis consideratio*, i.e., ratiocination or rational discourse.
29. *Intellectus consideratio*, i.e., intellectual intuition.

endeavors in all sciences has for its end the knowledge of divine science.

Now . . . the reason proceeds sometimes from one to another according to reality, as when demonstration is made through causes or through extrinsic effects—by composing indeed when proceeding from causes to effects, resolving when proceeding from effects to causes, for causes are simpler than effects and more immovably and uniformly permanent. The ultimate term of resolution in this procedure therefore is attained when the reason arrives at the supreme and simplest causes, which are the separated substances.

Sometimes, however, the process is from one thing to another according to reason, as when the advance is made according to intrinsic causes. This is by a method of composing, when from the most universal forms the reason proceeds to those more particular. But it is a method of resolving when the process is reversed, since the more universal is the simpler. Those things are in the highest degree universal, however, which are common to all beings, and therefore the ultimate term in this process of resolution is the consideration of being and of those things which pertain to being as such.

Now these are the very things of which divine science treats . . ., to wit, separated substances and the principles common to all beings. Hence it is evident that its consideration is preeminently intellectual. So too it follows that divine science confers principles upon all the other sciences, inasmuch as intellectual consideration is, in the order of reason, the principle on whose account divine science is called "first philosophy." And yet this science is learned after physics, inasmuch as intellectual consideration is the terminus of the rational. Wherefore divine science is called "metaphysics," as though one were to say "trans-physics," because it arises by way of resolution after physics.

3. THE WHOLE OF METAPHYSICS IS ORDERED TO THE KNOWLEDGE OF GOD[30]

Now since all creatures, even those devoid of intelligence, are directed to God as their last end and all reach this end so far as they have some share of likeness to Him, the intellectual creature attains to Him in a special way through its proper operation, namely, by understanding Him. This then must be the end of the intellectual creature: to know God.

For, as was shown above,[31] God is the end of each thing, and hence each thing, to the greatest extent possible to it, intends to be united to God as its last end. But a thing is more closely united to God by attaining in some way to His very substance (and this occurs when it has some cognition of that substance) than by simply attaining some likeness of Him. Therefore the intellectual substance tends to the knowledge of God as its last end.

Again. The operation proper to a thing is its end, for it is the thing's second perfection. Thus, that which is well conditioned for its proper operation is said to be fit and good. Now intellection *(intelligere)* is the proper operation of the intellectual substance, and consequently is its end. Therefore, whatever is most perfect in this operation is its last end; especially so in those operations, such as understanding and sensing, which are not directed to some product.[32] And since operations of this kind are specified by their objects, being known also through them, it follows necessarily that the more perfect the object of any such operation, the more perfect is the operation itself. Consequently the act of intellecting the most

---

30. This section comprises the whole of Chapter XXV in Book III of the *Summa Contra Gentiles:* "That to Know God Is the End of Every Intellectual Substance."
31. Chap. XVII.
32. I.e., in immanent operations, which do not issue in effects outside their efficient causes but remain in those causes and perfect them.

perfect intelligible object, namely God, is the most perfect act in the genus of the operation called "understanding" *(intelligere)*. Therefore to know God by an act of intellection is the last end of every intellectual substance.

Someone might however say that the last end of an intellectual substance consists indeed in intellecting the best intelligible object, but that what is the best intelligible object for this or that intellectual substance is not absolutely the best intelligible, and that the higher the intellectual substance, the higher is its best intelligible. So that perhaps the highest created intellectual substance has for its best intelligible object that which is best absolutely, and its happiness will consist in knowing God, whereas the happiness of any lower intellectual substance will consist in knowing some lower intelligible object, which however will be the highest reality known by it. And above all, in view of the weakness of the human intellect, it would seem not to be in its power to apprehend that which is absolutely the best intelligible thing; the human intellect being as well adapted for knowing the supremely intelligible "as the owl's eye for seeing the sun."[33]

It is evident nevertheless that the end of any intellectual substance, even the lowest, is to know God. For it was shown above[34] that God is the last end toward which all things tend. And although it is the lowest in the order of intellectual substances, the human intellect is superior to all things devoid of intellect. Since then a more noble substance has not a less noble end, God Himself will be the end also of the human intellect. Now, as we have shown, every intelligent being attains to its last end by understanding it. Therefore the human intellect attains to God as its end by understanding Him.

Again. Just as things devoid of intellect tend to God as their end by way of assimilation, so do intellectual substances by way of knowledge, as is evident from what has been said. Now, although things lacking intellect tend toward a likeness to their proximate

33. Cf. Aristotle, *Metaph.*, II (α), 1 (993b 9).
34. Chap. XVII.

agent causes, the intention of nature does not rest there but has for its end a likeness to the highest good, as we have proved.[35] Yet such things are able to attain to this likeness in a most imperfect manner. Therefore, however little be the knowledge of God to which the intellect is able to attain, this will be the intellect's last end, rather than a perfect knowledge of lower intelligibles.

Moreover. Everything desires most of all its last end. But the human intellect desires, loves and enjoys the knowledge of divine things, though it can grasp but little about them, more than the perfect knowledge which it has of the lowest things. Man's last end therefore is to understand God in some way.

Further. Everything tends to a likeness of God as its own end. Therefore that whereby a thing is most of all likened to God is its last end. Now the intellectual creature is especially likened to God in that it is intellectual, for this likeness belongs to it above other creatures, and this includes all other likenesses. And in this particular kind of likeness it is more like God in understanding actually than in understanding "habitually" *(in habitu),* or in understanding potentially. For God is always understanding actually, as was proved in the First Book.[36] And as regards what the intellect understands actually, it is by apprehending God Himself that it is in the highest mode likened to Him, for God Himself, in knowing Himself, knows all other things, as was proved also in the First Book.[37] To understand God is then the last end of every intellectual substance.

Again. That which is lovable only because of another thing is for the sake of that which is lovable solely on its own account; for it is impossible to go on indefinitely in the appetite of nature since nature's desire would then be in vain, and it is impossible to pass through an infinite number of things. But all sciences, arts, and powers of a practical nature are lovable only for the sake of

35. Chap. XIX.
36. *CG* I, 56.
37. *Ibid.,* chap. 49.

something else, because their end is not to know but to operate. Speculative sciences, on the other hand, are lovable for their own sake, since their end is the very act of knowing. Nor, with the exception of speculative thought, is there any action in human life that is not directed to some other end than knowledge as such. Even playful actions, seemingly done without purpose, have a certain end due to them, namely, to provide mental relaxation somehow or other, so that afterwards we may become more fit for studious occupations; were play desirable for its own sake, then it would always be in order; which is incongruous. So the practical arts are ordered to the speculative arts, and likewise every human operation to intellectual, speculative operation as its end. Now in all sciences and arts that are mutually ordered the last end seems to belong to the one from which the others derive their rules and principles. Thus the art of sailing (to which the ship's purpose, namely its use, pertains) provides rules and principles to the art of ship building. And such is the relation of first philosophy to other speculative sciences, since all others depend on it inasmuch as they derive their principles from it and are directed by it in defending those principles. Moreover, first philosophy itself, as a whole, is ordered to the knowledge of God as its last end, and for this reason is given the name also of "divine science."[38] Therefore the last end of all human knowledge and activity is the knowledge of God.

Further. In all mutually ordered agents and movers, the end of the first agent and mover must be the end of all, just as the end of the commander-in-chief is the end of all who are soldiering under him. Now, of all the parts of man the intellect is the highest mover, for it moves the appetite by proposing its object to it; and the intellective appetite, or the will, moves the sensitive appetites, namely, the irascible and the concupiscible. And so it is that we do not obey concupiscence unless the will commands, while the sensitive appetite, when the will has given its consent, moves the

38. Aristotle, *Metaph.*, I (A), 2 (983a 6).

body. Therefore the end of the intellect is the end of all human actions. Now "truth is the intellect's end and its good,"[39] and consequently its last end is the First Truth. Therefore the last end of the
whole man, and of all his deeds and desires, is to know the First
Truth, which is God.

Moreover. The desire to know the causes of the things they see
is naturally present in all men; and so through wondering at the
things they saw, whose causes were hidden from them, men first
began to philosophize, and when they had discovered the cause
they were at rest. Nor does inquiry cease until the first cause is attained: "Then do we deem ourselves to know perfectly, when we
know the first cause."[40] Therefore man naturally desires as his last
end to know the first cause. But God is the first cause of all things.
Therefore man's last end is to know God.

Again. Man naturally desires to know the cause of any known
effect. But the human intellect knows universal being. Therefore it
naturally desires to know its cause, which is God alone, as was
proved in the Second Book.[41] Now one has not attained to one's
last end until the natural desire is at rest. Hence for man's happiness,
which is his last end, no intellectual knowledge whatever suffices
except the knowledge of God, which terminates his natural desire
as his last end. The knowledge of God is itself therefore man's
ultimate end.

Further. A body that tends by its natural appetite to its proper
place is moved all the more vehemently and rapidly the nearer it
approaches its end. Hence Aristotle proves that a natural straight
movement cannot be toward an indefinite point, because it then
would not be moved afterward more than before.[42] Consequently
that which tends more vehemently to a thing afterward than before
is not moved toward an indefinite point but toward something

39. Aristotle, *Eth. Nicom.,* VI, 2 (1139a 27).
40. Aristotle, *Metaph.,* I (A), 3 (983a 25).
41. *CG* II, 25.

fixed. Now this we find in the desire of knowledge, for the more one knows, the greater is one's desire to know. Hence man's natural desire for knowledge tends to a definite end. This, however, can be none other than the highest thing knowable, which is God. Therefore the knowledge of God is man's last end.

Now the last end of man and of any intellectual substance is called happiness or beatitude, for it is this which every intellectual substance desires as its last end and for its own sake alone. Therefore the ultimate beatitude or happiness of every intellectual substance is to know God.

Wherefore it is said (Matt. 5:8): "Blessed are the clean of heart for they shall see God"; and (Jo. 17:3): "This is eternal life, that they may know thee, the only true God." Aristotle agrees with this judgment also when he says that man's ultimate happiness is speculative, and this with regard to the highest object of speculation.[43]

42. Cf. De Coelo, 1, 8 (277a 18ff.).
43. Cf. Eth. Nicom., X, 7 (1177a 18).